The Future of Food

Other Books of Related Interest

Opposing Viewpoints Series

Capitalism
Genetic Engineering and Gene Therapy
The Politics of Climate

At Issue Series

Can Diets Be Harmful?
Childhood Obesity
Food Security
Wellness Culture

Current Controversies Series

Agriculture
Attacks on Science
Fair Trade
The Industrial Food Complex

> “Congress shall make no law … abridging the freedom of speech, or of the press.”
>
> *First Amendment to the U.S. Constitution*

The basic foundation of our democracy is the First Amendment guarantee of freedom of expression. The Opposing Viewpoints series is dedicated to the concept of this basic freedom and the idea that it is more important to practice it than to enshrine it.

The Future of Food

Garrett Winter, Book Editor

Published in 2025 by Greenhaven Publishing, LLC
2544 Clinton Street,
Buffalo NY 14224

First Edition

Articles in Greenhaven Publishing anthologies are often edited for length to meet page requirements. In addition, original titles of these works are changed to clearly present the main thesis and to explicitly indicate the author's opinion. Every effort is made to ensure that Greenhaven Publishing accurately reflects the original intent of the authors. Every effort has been made to trace the owners of the copyrighted material.

Cover image: kung_tom/Shutterstock.com

Cataloging-in-Publication Data
Names: Winter, Garrett, editor.
Title: The future of food / edited by Garrett Winter.
Description: First edition. | New York : Greenhaven Publishing, 2026. | Series: Opposing viewpoints | Includes index.
Identifiers: ISBN 9781534510210 (pbk.) | ISBN 9781534510227 (library bound)
Subjects: LCSH: Food security--Juvenile literature. | Food supply--Juvenile literature. | Sustainable agriculture--Juvenile literature. | Food--Environmental aspects--Juvenile literature.
Classification: LCC HD9000.5 F88 2026 | DDC 338.19--dc23

Manufactured in the United States of America

Website: http://greenhavenpublishing.com

Contents

The Importance of Opposing Viewpoints 11
Introduction 14

Chapter 1: Will There Be Enough Food to Feed the Planet in the Future?

Chapter Preface 20

1. Climate Change Is Affecting Crop Yields 22
   Deepak Ray
2. Rising Temperatures Increase Global Food Insecurity 28
   World Bank Group
3. Hunger Numbers Stubbornly High Amid Global Crises 33
   World Health Organization
4. Water is Crucial to Food Production 43
   Claudia Ringler and Jenna Wilf

Periodical and Internet Sources Bibliography 48

Chapter 2: What Is the Future of Farming?

Chapter Preface 50

1. Behavioral Science Can Help Optimize Farm Yields 52
   Kaylee Somerville
2. Agricultural Subsidies Must Change With the Times 57
   Ashok Gulati
3. Locally Sourced Produce Is Beneficial to All of Us 64
   Ruth Linton
4. Digital Technology is Integral to the Future of Food 73
   Lutz Goedde, Joshua Katz, Alexandre Ménard, and Julien Revellat

Periodical and Internet Sources Bibliography 87

Chapter 3: What is the Future of Meat?

Chapter Preface 89

1. Innovative Methods are Needed to Combat Livestock-Induced Climate Change 91
   Kristin Houser
2. Corporations are Exploring Sustainable Alternatives to Traditional Meat Production 97
   Kara Baskin
3. Lab Grown Meat as the Future of Food is Still a Long Way Off 104
   Keena Alwahaidi
4. The Demand for Meat is Driving Deforestation in Brazil 109
   Angela Guerrero and Malika Virah-Sawmy
5. The Safety of Lab-Grown Meat Is a Serious Concern 114
   Jaydee Hanson and Julia Ranney
6. Lab-Grown Products Offer a Promising Alternative to Traditional Meat 123
   William Brangham and Mike Fritz
7. Cultured Meat Offers a New Role for Traditional Farms 130
   Innovation for Agriculture

Periodical and Internet Sources Bibliography 136

Chapter 4: Will Food Continue to Be Used as a Weapon of War?

Chapter Preface 138

1. Political Actions are the Chief Cause of Famine 139
   Heather Stephenson
2. Hunger Is a Brutal Weapon 144
   Ulriikka Myöhänen

3. Weaponization of Food Doesn't Always Result in Victory **153**
Greg Kennedy

4. Peace Is the Only Way to Prevent Famine in War-Torn Countries **157**
The United Nations

Periodical and Internet Sources Bibliography **162**

For Further Discussion **164**

Organizations to Contact **166**

Bibliography of Books **171**

Index **173**

The Importance of Opposing Viewpoints

Perhaps every generation experiences a period in time in which the populace seems especially polarized, starkly divided on the important issues of the day and gravitating toward the far ends of the political spectrum and away from a consensus-facilitating middle ground. The world that today's students are growing up in and that they will soon enter into as active and engaged citizens is deeply fragmented in just this way. Issues relating to terrorism, immigration, women's rights, minority rights, race relations, health care, taxation, wealth and poverty, the environment, policing, military intervention, the proper role of government—in some ways, perennial issues that are freshly and uniquely urgent and vital with each new generation—are currently roiling the world.

If we are to foster a knowledgeable, responsible, active, and engaged citizenry among today's youth, we must provide them with the intellectual, interpretive, and critical-thinking tools and experience necessary to make sense of the world around them and of the all-important debates and arguments that inform it. After all, the outcome of these debates will in large measure determine the future course, prospects, and outcomes of the world and its peoples, particularly its youth. If they are to become successful members of society and productive and informed citizens, students need to learn how to evaluate the strengths and weaknesses of someone else's arguments, how to sift fact from opinion and fallacy, and how to test the relative merits and validity of their own opinions against the known facts and the best possible available information. The landmark series Opposing Viewpoints has been providing students with just such critical-thinking skills and exposure to the debates surrounding society's most urgent contemporary issues for many years, and it continues to serve this essential role with undiminished commitment, care, and rigor.

The key to the series's success in achieving its goal of sharpening students' critical-thinking and analytic skills resides in its title—

Opposing Viewpoints. In every intriguing, compelling, and engaging volume of this series, readers are presented with the widest possible spectrum of distinct viewpoints, expert opinions, and informed argumentation and commentary, supplied by some of today's leading academics, thinkers, analysts, politicians, policy makers, economists, activists, change agents, and advocates. Every opinion and argument anthologized here is presented objectively and accorded respect. There is no editorializing in any introductory text or in the arrangement and order of the pieces. No piece is included as a "straw man," an easy ideological target for cheap point-scoring. As wide and inclusive a range of viewpoints as possible is offered, with no privileging of one particular political ideology or cultural perspective over another. It is left to each individual reader to evaluate the relative merits of each argument—as he or she sees it, and with the use of ever-growing critical-thinking skills—and grapple with his or her own assumptions, beliefs, and perspectives to determine how convincing or successful any given argument is and how the reader's own stance on the issue may be modified or altered in response to it.

This process is facilitated and supported by volume, chapter, and selection introductions that provide readers with the essential context they need to begin engaging with the spotlighted issues, with the debates surrounding them, and with their own perhaps shifting or nascent opinions on them. In addition, guided reading and discussion questions encourage readers to determine the authors' point of view and purpose, interrogate and analyze the various arguments and their rhetoric and structure, evaluate the arguments' strengths and weaknesses, test their claims against available facts and evidence, judge the validity of the reasoning, and bring into clearer, sharper focus the reader's own beliefs and conclusions and how they may differ from or align with those in the collection or those of their classmates.

Research has shown that reading comprehension skills improve dramatically when students are provided with compelling, intriguing, and relevant "discussable" texts. The subject matter of these collections could not be more compelling, intriguing, or urgently relevant to today's students and the world they are poised to inherit. The anthologized articles and the reading and discussion questions that are included with them also provide the basis for stimulating, lively, and passionate classroom debates. Students who are compelled to anticipate objections to their own argument and identify the flaws in those of an opponent read more carefully, think more critically, and steep themselves in relevant context, facts, and information more thoroughly. In short, using discussable text of the kind provided by every single volume in the Opposing Viewpoints series encourages close reading, facilitates reading comprehension, fosters research, strengthens critical thinking, and greatly enlivens and energizes classroom discussion and participation. The entire learning process is deepened, extended, and strengthened.

For all of these reasons, Opposing Viewpoints continues to be exactly the right resource at exactly the right time—when we most need to provide readers with the critical-thinking tools and skills that will not only serve them well in school but also in their careers and their daily lives as decision-making family members, community members, and citizens. This series encourages respectful engagement with and analysis of opposing viewpoints and fosters a resulting increase in the strength and rigor of one's own opinions and stances. As such, it helps make readers "future ready," and that readiness will pay rich dividends for the readers themselves, for the citizenry, for our society, and for the world at large.

Introduction

> *"When we look at history, food is consistently one of, if not the primary driver, in shifts in human behaviour."*
>
> *— Jenny Dorsey*

It is no stretch to say that the future of food has already arrived. One could make a plausible argument that this future began 10,000 years ago, when humans first began modifying plants, animals, and microbes in order to produce more desirable outcomes. With the discovery of DNA, scientists were given a key by which they could produce better edible products. Today, scientists have as much to do with the production of food as do farmers.

What we now know as genetic engineering of plants and foods began in the 1970s. In the 1980s, the U.S. Food and Drug Administration (FDA) greenlighted the first consumer genetically modified organism (GMO), which was insulin that was created in the laboratory. The 1980s also saw the introduction of the first GMO plant approved for human consumption, the "Flavr Savr" tomato.

GMOs work by introducing specific genes from one organism into another to create a desired outcome, a trait that will improve the target organism. GMOs are advantageous in many ways. Scientists can create foods that are disease and drought resistant, that require fewer environmental resources such as water and fertilizer, and that grow more quickly. In addition, insect-resistant GMO crops require fewer pesticides.

With the creation of GMOs came controversy, as conspiracy theorists emerged. One such conspiracy theory involved genetically modified rice, also referred to as "golden rice." This fortified rice was developed to address a shortage of vitamin A, especially among women and children in poverty stricken nations. Critics have made all kinds of wild claims about golden rice, even though the scientific consensus is that it is safe to eat.

Conspiracy theories also abound concerning giant agricultural companies such as Monsanto and Syngenta. Such widespread theories suggest that GMOs are being systematically, knowingly, and maliciously introduced into the food supply either to enrich agribusinesses or to poison or control the population. Again, the scientific consensus is that genetically modified products are safe to eat. According to the Alliance for Science, "Governments everywhere employ strict biosafety protocols to ensure that any new GM [genetically modified] product poses no threat to human or animal health, or the environment. These protocols include laboratory and field tests that may span many years."

It is unsurprising that people do not completely trust what they do not understand. After all, the process for creating what some have disdainfully labeled "Frankenfoods" is not a simple one, nor is it simply understood. GMOs are created by transferring genes from one organism to another through recombinant DNA technology. The process begins with identifying a desired trait, isolating the gene responsible for that trait, and then inserting that gene into the DNA of the organism to be modified. As Pamela C. Ronald and Raoul W. Adamchak write in their book, *Tomorrow's Table*, "Campaigns to ban genetically engineered crops reflect a general anxiety about plant genetics and a distrust of established institutions." They add that "Mistrust of science for ideological or political purposes has muddied the debates surrounding genetically engineered crops."

A major part of the future of GM foods is a gene editing tool named CRISPR that was developed in the early 21st century. CRISPR (Clustered Regularly Interspaced Short Palindromic Repeats) gene editing allows scientists to modify DNA sequences with precision. It works by using RNA to find a target DNA sequence. Then, using a protein, it severs the DNA at that location. The cell's natural DNA repair system takes over, either by correcting the break with a new DNA sequence or simply by repairing the break, which can lead to changes in the DNA sequencing.

If the above seems too complicated, we can think of CRISPR as a type of "genetic scissors." Here's how *World Economic Forum* Senior Writer Douglas Broom envisions a gene editing future: "Imagine if scientists could manipulate cells at the molecular level, remove molecules, add them, or fuse them together. How could they change the world?"

One limitation of older GMO technology is that more than one plant's DNA needs to interact with the host. Gene editing requires no second or third organism. Instead, this process edits the DNA of a single plant. This creates a more homogenous, more controlled outcome.

While CRISPR has the potential to change the genomic landscape of agriculture, how CRISPR edited crops will be regulated will determine the future of this technology. The United States, for example, has deregulated CRISPR created crops because of their homogenous quality. But other countries are more skeptical.

Many believe the benefits of gene edited food are so great on a practical level that they cannot be ignored. Douglas Broom provides an example: "Any parent will tell you how hard it can be to persuade children to eat green vegetables and salads. But CRISPR is coming to the rescue, making healthy foods taste better by dialing down the bitterness in many vegetables and enhancing the flavour of fruit." Gene editing, Broom says, is also able to create crops that can flourish in harsh conditions and that can withstand the impact of the climate crisis.

If genetic engineering can eventually produce safe crops that are more insect resistant, more nutrient-enriched, and more plentiful, can science begin to eliminate food insecurity across the globe? The answer is more complex than one might think. Even with over half a century of innovation in the field of genetic modification, food insecurity is increasing rather than diminishing. According to a 2023 United Nations report, "Over 122 million more people are facing hunger in the world since 2019." The report finds that "approximately 2.4 billion individuals, largely women and residents of rural areas, did not have consistent access to nutritious, safe, and sufficient food in 2022."

Food and Water Watch, an organization that works to protect food, water, and air, paints a somewhat bleak picture when it comes to using new technologies to feed the world. They write that "Genetically modified foods…are another tool industrial agriculture uses to control our food system. GMOs aren't about feeding the world, they're about corporate profits."

Feeding the planet in the 21st century and beyond is not just about producing more food. According to "A Well-Fed World," another organization dedicated to global food security, hunger relief, and climate advocacy, "On paper, the world has enough calories to feed 10+ billion people (global population exceeded 8.2 billion in February 2025)." Food waste, warfare, poor distribution methods, and numerous other factors all contribute to this surplus of food not reaching hungry mouths. It will be the work of future scientists, governments, and more, to see that the worsening problem of food insecurity can be reversed.

Opposing Viewpoints: The Future of Food presents a wide range of viewpoints that define and debate various concepts concerning the production, distribution, and use of food. The essays that follow demonstrate that our understanding of food production is still developing, and that the history of food around the world is still being written.

Chapter 1

Will There Be Enough Food to Feed the Planet in the Future?

Chapter Preface

As the proverb says, "Waste not, want not." According to the United Nations, "Globally, around 13.2 percent of food produced is lost between harvest and retail, while an estimated 19 percent of total global food production is wasted in households, in the food service and in retail all togethert." That adds up to just under one-third of all food products that never make it into a mouth.

This is a challenging statistic to study when coupled with statistics regarding food insecurity. For example, according to the U.S. Department of Agriculture (USDA), 13.5 percent of U.S. households experienced food insecurity in 2023. The government defines this as "households [that] were uncertain of having or unable to acquire enough food to meet the needs of all their members because they had insufficient money or other resources for food." Five percent of families had what the government called "very low food security," meaning that "normal eating patterns of one or more household members were disrupted and food intake was reduced at times during the year because they had insufficient money or other resources for food."

And yet many food secure families throw out bushels of food per year. There are ways to prevent or at least extend the life of most of these foods, but many families don't necessarily make the effort. They can always buy more food from the grocery store.

A similar pattern occurs in the food industry. About 30 percent of U.S. grocery store food ends up in the trash. This amounts to billions of pounds per year.

Many states have enacted legislation to curb food waste. California has "perhaps the most progressive and strictest of the states with Food Waste Laws. [It] requires all its inhabitants, whether they be commercial businesses, public institutes or private residents to separate their green waste," according to writer Annie Wilhelm. Connecticut passed a "Commercial Organics Recycling

Law" in 2022. The law mandates that if a business produces over 26 tons (23.6 metric tons) of organic waste per year, they will have to separate their food waste to be disposed of at an organic waste facility. Maryland, Massachusetts, New York, Rhode Island and Washington are among other states with food waste laws.

Some corporations are also trying to tackle food waste. A fairly recent startup called "Too Good to Go" connects food shoppers with restaurants and supermarkets that have leftovers at the end of the day. Using an app, customers can purchase the leftover food at a greatly reduced rate and pick it up before the establishment closes for the day. Whole Foods, for example, has a nationwide program with Too Good to Go.

Despite all of the positive efforts, tons and tons of edible food is wasted every day in the United States. It will take a serious, nationwide effort to combat food waste, but such an endeavor is not currently on the horizon.

The viewpoints presented in this chapter discuss the problem of food insecurity from a variety of angles. As you read each viewpoint, consider what you have learned about food waste and its impact on this issue as well.

Viewpoint 1

"Our analysis showed that climate change has already affected crop yields around the world. There were variations between locations and among crops, but when all of these different results were totaled, we found yields of some important global staples were already declining."

Climate Change Is Affecting Crop Yields

Deepak Ray

In this viewpoint, Deepak Ray discusses the impact of climate change on global crop productivity and food security, highlighting a study conducted by researchers from the University of Minnesota over four years. It focuses on the top ten crops that provide the majority of food calories, revealing that while some crops have seen yield increases in certain regions, overall climate change is leading to declines in important "staple" crops. Deepak Ray is a Senior Scientist with IonE's Global Landscapes Initiative. He conducts research on local to global scale food security. His mission is to help non-governmental agencies, industries, international organizations, and governments make more informed policies and to explore ways to overcome the challenges faced in the agriculture and food security sectors.

As you read, consider the following questions:

1. According to Ray, what crops have benefited from climate change?
2. Conversely, what crops are doing worse?
3. According to Ray, what countries have been most affected by reduced crop yields?

Farmers are used to dealing with weather, but climate change is making it harder by altering temperature and rainfall patterns, as in this year's unusually cool and wet spring in the central U.S. In a recently published study, I worked with other scientists to see whether climate change was measurably affecting crop productivity and global food security.

To analyze these questions, a team of researchers led by the University of Minnesota's Institute on the Environment spent four years collecting information on crop productivity from around the world. We focused on the top 10 global crops that provide the bulk of consumable food calories: Maize (corn), rice, wheat, soybeans, oil palm, sugarcane, barley, rapeseed (canola), cassava and sorghum. Roughly 83 percent of consumable food calories come from just these 10 sources. Other than cassava and oil palm, all are important U.S. crops.

We found that climate change has affected yields in many places. Not all of the changes are negative: Some crop yields have increased in some locations. Overall, however, climate change is reducing global production of staples such as rice and wheat. And when we translated crop yields into consumable calories – the actual food on people's plates – we found that climate change is already shrinking food supplies, particularly in food-insecure developing countries.

Adding up local trends

The first thing we needed to understand was how temperature and precipitation influenced crop productivity in many locations. To do this, we analyzed data from up to 20,000 counties and districts

Is There a Global Food Shortage? What's Causing Hunger, Famine and Rising Food Costs Around the World

Why We Don't Have a Global Food Shortage

There is no global food shortage because we produce more than enough food to feed everyone in the world. We produce so much food globally yet one–third of it – 1.3 billion tons – is wasted. According to the U.N. Food and Agriculture Organization (FAO), all that wasted food is enough to feed 1.26 billion people: almost twice the number of undernourished people across the globe.

So, if there's enough food for everyone in the world, why do some countries face food shortages? It's mostly due to a lack of access to food, technology and resilient food production systems.

What Causes Food Shortages Around the World?

Some countries and regions can't provide enough food for their people. Why does this happen?

around the world to see how crop yields varied in each place with changes in precipitation and temperature.

Once we had constructed an empirical model connecting crop yield to weather variations at each location, we could use it to assess how much yields had changed from what we would have expected to see if average weather patterns had not changed. The difference between what we would have predicted, based on the counterfactual weather, and what actually occurred reflects the influence of climate change.

Our analysis showed that climate change has already affected crop yields around the world. There were variations between locations and among crops, but when all of these different results

Without enough: People with skills like scientists, farmers, and logistics and transport experts who uphold efficient food systems, financial capital, and environmental resources like arable land and water needed to grow food, a country may be unable to provide enough food for its people.

In low-income countries especially, a lack of resources can also lead to high rates of food loss during the early stages of growth, harvest and storage. For example, poor storage can lead to infestations or mold that ruin food before it can be eaten.

Or, a country might produce or be able to import enough food for its population but shocks like climate disasters or political upheaval prevent the equitable distribution of food to vulnerable or isolated communities. Those communities then lose access to food and can experience a shortage. And bigger disruptors, like war, can stop trade or destroy food systems entirely.

"Is There a Global Food Shortage? What's Causing Hunger, Famine and Rising Food Costs Around the World" by World Food Program USA, Published November 16, 2023.

were totaled, we found yields of some important global staples were already declining. For example, we estimated that climate change was reducing global rice yields by 0.3% and wheat yields by 0.9% on average each year.

In contrast, some more drought-tolerant crops have benefited from climate change. Yields of sorghum, which many people in the developing world use as a food grain, have increased by 0.7% in sub-Saharan Africa and 0.9% yearly in western, southern and southeastern Asia due to climate shifts since the 1970s.

Climate change is boosting maize (corn) yields in parts of the U.S., Latin America and Asia, but sharply reducing them elsewhere. (Ray et al., 2019, CC BY)

A mixed US picture

In the United States corn and soybeans are important cash crops, with a combined value of more than US$90 billion in 2017. We found that climate change is causing a small net increase in yields of these crops – on average, about 0.1% and 3.7% respectively each year.

But these numbers reflect both gains and losses. In some Corn Belt states, such as Indiana and Illinois, climate change is shaving up to 8% off of annual corn yields. At the same time, it has boosted annual yields in Iowa and Minnesota by approximately 2.8%. All four of these states now have slightly warmer and wetter corn growing seasons, but Indiana and Illinois have seen larger increases in warming and smaller increases in moisture compared to Iowa and Minnesota.

Our maps track these changes down to the county level. In eastern Iowa, Illinois and Indiana, climate change has been reducing corn yields even as it boosts them to the northwest in Minnesota and North Dakota. We see similar patterns for soybean farming: Reductions are moving up from the south and east parts of the country, where slightly more warming has occurred than in states farther north. Climate change is also reducing overall yields of other important crops, such as wheat and barley.

From harvests to meals

While these impacts on crop yields are notable in themselves, we had to go a step farther to understand how they could affect global food security. Humans eat food, not crop yields, so we needed to determine how climate change was affecting supplies of consumable food calories. In its most recent assessment report, the Intergovernmental Panel on Climate Change recognized that this question had not yet been answered and was critical to building a strong case for climate change action.

Our study showed that climate change is reducing consumable food calories by around 1% yearly for the top 10 global crops. This may sound small, but it represents some 35 trillion calories each year. That's enough to provide more than 50 million people with a daily diet of over 1,800 calories – the level that the U.N. Food and Agriculture Organization identifies as essential to avoid food deprivation or undernourishment.

What's more, we found that decreases in consumable food calories are already occurring in roughly half of the world's food insecure countries, which have high rates of undernourishment, child stunting and wasting, and mortality among children under age 5 due to lack of sufficient food. For example, in India annual food calories have declined by 0.8% annually and in Nepal they have fallen by 2.2% annually.

Reductions are also occurring in southern African countries, including Malawi, Mozambique and Zimbabwe. We even found losses in some rich industrialized nations, such as Australia, France and Germany.

Rich countries can work their way out of food calorie shortages by importing food. But poorer countries may need help. Short-term strategies could include using our findings to breed or increase cultivation of crops that are resilient to or even benefit from climate change. Farming techniques and agriculture policies can also help small-scale farmers increase crop yields.

The fact that world hunger has started to rise after a decade-long decline is alarming. In the long run, wealthy and developing countries alike will have to find ways to produce food in a changing climate. I hope this will lead to a rethinking of the entire food system, from diets to food waste, and to more sustainable techniques for feeding the world.

> *"Without solutions, falling crop yields, especially in the world's most food-insecure regions, will push more people into poverty – an estimated 43 million people in Africa alone could fall below the poverty line by 2030 as a result."*

Rising Temperatures Increase Global Food Insecurity

World Bank Group

This viewpoint by the World Bank Group discusses the significant impact of climate change on global food security, highlighting that the number of people facing acute food insecurity has surged in the current decade, with climate change exacerbating this surge through extreme weather patterns and rising food prices. The viewpoint argues that the global food system contributes heavily to greenhouse gas emissions and that vulnerable populations, particularly in Sub-Saharan Africa and South Asia, are most affected by crop failures and hunger. The authors suggest potential adaptation strategies for agriculture, while also detailing the World Bank's initiatives to support climate-smart agriculture and improve resilience in food systems. World Bank Group is an organization dedicated to ending extreme poverty and boosting shared prosperity on a livable planet.

As you read, consider the following questions:

1. What factors besides climate change have increased food insecurity in the 2020s?
2. How can food producers combat climate change?
3. According to the World Bank Group, what have they been doing to aid food production on a global scale?

How is climate change affecting global food security today and what can we expect in the future? We asked William R. Sutton, Global Lead for Climate Smart Agriculture for the World Bank, to explain the potential impacts of a warmer world on the food system.

What is the state of global food security today, and what is the role of climate change?

The number of people suffering acute food insecurity increased from 135 million in 2019 to 345 million in 82 countries by June 2022, as the war in Ukraine, supply chain disruptions, and the continued economic fallout of the COVID-19 pandemic pushed food prices to all-time highs.

Global food insecurity had already been rising, due in large part to climate phenomena. Global warming is influencing weather patterns, causing heat waves, heavy rainfall, and droughts. Rising food commodity prices in 2021 were a major factor in pushing approximately 30 million additional people in low-income countries toward food insecurity.

At the same time, the way that food is often produced today is a big part of the problem. It's recently been estimated that the global food system is responsible for about a third of greenhouse gas emissions—second only to the energy sector; it is the number one source of methane and biodiversity loss.

It's recently been estimated that the global food system is responsible for about a third of greenhouse gas emissions—second only to the energy sector; it is the number one source of methane and biodiversity loss.

Who is most affected by climate impacts on food security?

About 80% of the global population most at risk from crop failures and hunger from climate change are in Sub-Saharan Africa, South Asia, and Southeast Asia, where farming families are disproportionally poor and vulnerable. A severe drought caused by an El Nino weather pattern or climate change can push millions more people into poverty. This is true even in places like the Philippines and Vietnam, which have relatively high incomes, but where farmers often live at the edge of poverty and food price increases have an outsized impact on poor urban consumers.

How might climate change affect farming and food security in the future?

Up to a certain point, rising temperatures and CO_2 can be beneficial for crops. But rising temperatures also accelerate evapotranspiration from plants and soils, and there must also be enough water for crops to thrive.

For areas of the world that are already water-constrained, climate change will increasingly cause adverse impacts on agricultural production through diminishing water supplies, increases in extreme events like floods and severe storms, heat stress, and increased prevalence of pests and diseases.

Above a certain point of warming -- and particularly above an increase of 2 degrees Celsius in average global temperatures – it becomes increasingly more difficult to adapt and increasingly more expensive. In countries where temperatures are already extremely high, such as the Sahel belt of Africa or South Asia, rising temperatures could have a more immediate effect on crops such as wheat that are less heat tolerant.

Without solutions, falling crop yields, especially in the world's most food-insecure regions, will push more people into poverty

– an estimated 43 million people in Africa alone could fall below the poverty line by 2030 as a result.

How can agriculture adapt to climate change?

It's possible to reduce emissions and become more resilient, but doing so often requires major social, economic, and technological change. There are a few key strategies:

Use water more efficiently and effectively, combined with policies to manage demand. Building more irrigation infrastructure may not be a solution if future water supply proves to be inadequate to supply the irrigation systems—which our research has shown may indeed be the case for some countries. Other options include better management of water demand as well as the use of advanced water accounting systems and technologies to assess the amount of water available, including soil moisture sensors and satellite evapotranspiration measurements. Such measures can facilitate techniques such as alternate wetting and drying of rice paddies, which saves water and reduces methane emissions at the same time.

Switch to less-thirsty crops. For example, rice farmers could switch to crops that require less water such as maize or legumes. Doing so would also help reduce methane emissions, because rice is a major source of agri-food emissions. But a culture that has been growing and consuming rice for thousands of years may not so easily switch to another less thirsty, less emitting crop.

Improve soil health. This is hugely important. Increasing organic carbon in soil helps it better retain water and allows plants to access water more readily, increasing resilience to drought. It also provides more nutrients without requiring as much chemical fertilizer—which is a major source of emissions. Farmers can restore carbon that has been lost by not tilling soil and by using cover crops, particularly with large roots, in the rotation cycle rather than leaving fields fallow. Such nature-based solutions to environmental challenges could deliver 37% of climate change mitigation necessary to meet the goals of the Paris Agreement. But getting farmers to adopt these practices will take time, awareness-raising and training. In places where farm plots are small and farmers can't afford to let fields lie fallow or even rotate with leguminous crops, improving soil health could pose a challenge.

What is the World Bank doing to help countries build food security in the face of climate change?

The World Bank Group's Climate Change Action Plan (2021-2025) is stepping up support for climate-smart agriculture across the agriculture and food value chains and via policy and technological interventions to enhance productivity, improve resilience, and reduce GHG emissions. The Bank also helps countries tackle food loss and waste and manage flood and drought risks. For example, in Niger, a Bank-supported project aims to benefit 500,000 farmers and pastoralists in 44 communes through the distribution of improved, drought-tolerant seeds, more efficient irrigation, and expanded use of forestry for farming and conservation agriculture techniques. To date, the project has helped 336,518 farmers more sustainably manage their land and brought 79,938 hectares under more sustainable farming practices.

VIEWPOINT 3

> *"The lack of economic access to healthy diets also remains a critical issue, affecting over one-third of the global population."*

Hunger Numbers Stubbornly High Amid Global Crises

World Health Organization

This viewpoint discusses the State of Food Security and Nutrition in the World report, which reveals that approximately 733 million people faced hunger in 2023, indicating a significant setback in global efforts to achieve Zero Hunger by 2030. The report emphasizes the urgent need for increased financing and innovative solutions to transform food systems, address inequalities, and ensure access to nutritious food for all. The World Health Organization (WHO) is the United Nations agency dedicated to global health and safety.

As you read, consider the following questions:

1. Why has the U.N.'s goal of achieving zero hunger by 2030 suffered a significant setback?
2. How has the prevalence of adult obesity changed from 2012 to 2022?
3. What are the major factors contributing to food insecurity and malnutrition according to the report?

"Hunger numbers stubbornly high for three consecutive years as global crises deepen: UN report" by World Health Organization, July 24, 2024, Reprinted by permission.

Around 733 million people faced hunger in 2023, equivalent to one in eleven people globally and one in five in Africa, according to the latest State of Food Security and Nutrition in the World (SOFI) report published today by five United Nations specialized agencies.

The annual report, launched this year in the context of the G20 Global Alliance against Hunger and Poverty Task Force Ministerial Meeting in Brazil, warns that the world is falling significantly short of achieving Sustainable Development Goal (SDG) 2, Zero Hunger, by 2030. The report shows that the world has been set back 15 years, with levels of undernourishment comparable to those in 2008-2009.

Despite some progress in specific areas such as stunting and exclusive breastfeeding, an alarming number of people continue to face food insecurity and malnutrition as global hunger levels have plateaued for three consecutive years, with between 713 and 757 million people undernourished in 2023—approximately 152 million more than in 2019 when considering the mid-range (733 million).

Regional trends vary significantly: the percentage of the population facing hunger continues to rise in Africa (20.4 percent), remains stable in Asia (8.1 percent)—though still representing a significant challenge as the region is home to more than half of those facing hunger worldwide—and shows progress in Latin America (6.2 percent). From 2022 to 2023, hunger increased in Western Asia, the Caribbean, and most African subregions.

If current trends continue, about 582 million people will be chronically undernourished in 2030, half of them in Africa, warn the Food and Agriculture Organization of the United Nations (FAO), the International Fund for Agricultural Development (IFAD), the United Nations Children's Fund (UNICEF), the UN World Food Programme (WFP), and the World Health Organization (WHO). This projection closely resembles the levels seen in 2015 when the Sustainable

Development Goals were adopted, marking a concerning stagnation in progress.

Key findings beyond hunger

The report highlights that access to adequate food remains elusive for billions. In 2023, around 2.33 billion people globally faced moderate or severe food insecurity, a number that has not changed significantly since the sharp upturn in 2020, amid the COVID-19 pandemic. Among those, over 864 million people experienced severe food insecurity, going without food for an entire day or more at times. This number has remained stubbornly high since 2020 and while Latin America shows improvement, broader challenges persist, especially in Africa where 58 percent of the population is moderately or severely food insecure.

The lack of economic access to healthy diets also remains a critical issue, affecting over one-third of the global population. With new food price data and methodological improvements, the publication reveals that over 2.8 billion people were unable to afford a healthy diet in 2022. This disparity is most pronounced in low-income countries, where 71.5 percent of the population cannot afford a healthy diet, compared to 6.3 percent in high-income countries. Notably, the number dropped below pre-pandemic levels in Asia and in Northern America and Europe, while it increased substantially in Africa.

While progress has been made in increasing exclusive breastfeeding rates among infants to 48%, achieving global nutrition targets will be a challenge. Low birthweight prevalence has stagnated around 15%, and stunting among children under five, while declining to 22.3%, still falls short of achieving targets. Additionally, the prevalence of wasting among children has not seen significant improvement while anaemia in women aged 15 to 49 years has increased.

Similarly, new estimates of adult obesity show a steady increase over the last decade, from 12.1 percent (2012) to

15.8 percent (2022). Projections indicate that by 2030, the world will have more than 1.2 billion obese adults. The double burden of malnutrition – the co-existence of undernutrition together with overweight and obesity – has also surged globally across all age groups. Thinness and underweight have declined in the last two decades, while obesity has risen sharply.

These trends underscore the complex challenges of malnutrition in all its forms and the urgent need for targeted interventions as the world is not on track to reach any of the seven global nutrition targets by 2030, the five agencies indicate.

Food insecurity and malnutrition are worsening due to a combination of factors, including persisting food price inflation that continues to erode economic gains for many people in many countries. Major drivers like conflict, climate change, and economic downturns are becoming more frequent and severe. These issues, along with underlying factors such as unaffordable healthy diets, unhealthy food environments and persistent inequality, are now coinciding simultaneously, amplifying their individual effects.

Financing to end hunger

This year's report's theme "Financing to end hunger, food insecurity and all forms of malnutrition", emphasizes that achieving SDG 2 Zero Hunger requires a multi-faceted approach, including transforming and strengthening agrifood systems, addressing inequalities, and ensuring affordable and accessible healthy diets for all. It calls for increased and more cost-effective financing, with a clear and standardized definition of financing for food security and nutrition.

The heads of the five UN agencies, FAO Director-General QU Dongyu; IFAD President Alvaro Lario; UNICEF Executive Director Catherine Russell; WFP's Executive Director Cindy McCain; and WHO Director-General Dr. Tedros Adhanom Ghebreyesus write in the report's Foreword: "Estimating the gap in financing for food security and nutrition and mobilizing innovative ways of financing to bridge it must be among our top priorities. Policies, legislation and interventions to end hunger and ensure all people have access to safe, nutritious and sufficient food (SDG Target 2.1), and to end all forms of malnutrition (SDG Target 2.2) need significant resource mobilization. They are not only an investment in the future, but our obligation. We strive to guarantee the right to adequate food and nutrition of current and future generations".

As highlighted during a recent event in the High-Level Political Forum at UN headquarters in New York, the report underscores that the looming financing gap necessitates innovative, equitable solutions, particularly for countries facing high levels of hunger and malnutrition exacerbated by climate impacts.

Countries most in need of increased financing face significant challenges in access. Among the 119 low- and middle-income countries analyzed, approximately 63 percent have limited or moderate access to financing. Additionally, the majority of these countries (74 percent) are impacted by one or more major factors contributing to food insecurity and malnutrition. Coordinated efforts to harmonize data, increase risk tolerance, and enhance transparency are vital to bridge this gap and strengthen global food security and nutrition frameworks.

What they said

FAO Director-General, QU Dongyu: "Transforming agrifood systems is more critical than ever as we face the urgency of achieving the SDGs within six short years. FAO remains committed to supporting countries in their efforts to eradicate hunger and ensure food security for all. We will work together with all partners and with all approaches, including the G20 Global Alliance against Hunger and Poverty, to accelerate the needed change. Together, we must innovate and collaborate to build more efficient, inclusive, resilient, and sustainable agrifood systems that can better withstand future challenges for a better world."

IFAD President, Alvaro Lario: "The fastest route out of hunger and poverty is proven to be through investments in agriculture in rural areas. But the global and financial landscape has become far more complex since the Sustainable Development Goals were adopted in 2015. Ending hunger and malnutrition demands that we invest more - and more smartly. We must bring new money into the system from the private sector and recapture the pandemic-era appetite for ambitious global financial reform that gets cheaper financing to the countries who need it most."

UNICEF Executive Director, Catherine Russell: "Malnutrition affects a child's survival, physical growth, and brain development. Global child stunting rates have dropped by one third, or 55 million, in the last two decades, showing that investments in maternal and child nutrition pay off. Yet globally, one in four children under the age of five suffers from undernutrition, which can lead to long-term damage. We must urgently step-up financing to end child malnutrition. The world can and must do it. It is not only a moral imperative but also a sound investment in the future."

WFP Executive Director, Cindy McCain: "A future free from hunger is possible if we can rally the resources and the political will needed to invest in proven long-term solutions. I call on G20 leaders to follow Brazil's example and prioritize ambitious global action on hunger and poverty," said WFP Executive Director Cindy McCain. "We have the technologies and know-how to end food insecurity – but we urgently need the funds to invest in them at scale. WFP is ready to step up our collaboration with governments and partners to tackle the root causes of hunger, strengthen social safety nets and support sustainable development so every family can live in dignity."

WHO Director-General, Dr. Tedros Adhanom Ghebreyesus: "The progress we have made on reducing stunting and improving exclusive breastfeeding shows that the challenges we face are not insurmountable. We must use those gains as motivation to alleviate the suffering that millions of people around the world endure every day from hunger, food insecurity, unhealthy diets and malnutrition. The substantial investment required in healthy, safe and sustainably produced food is far less than the costs to economies and societies if we do nothing."

Notes to the editor: the SOFI report

The State of Food Security and Nutrition in the World is an annual report jointly prepared by the Food and Agriculture Organization of the United Nations (FAO), the International Fund for Agricultural Development (IFAD), the United Nations Children's Fund (UNICEF), the UN World Food Programme (WFP) and the World Health Organization (WHO).

Since 1999, it has monitored and analysed the world's progress towards ending hunger, achieving food security and improving nutrition. It also provides an in-depth analysis of key challenges for achieving these goals in the context of the 2030 Agenda for Sustainable Development. The report targets a wide audience, including policymakers, international organizations, academic institutions and the general public.

This year's theme is timely and relevant in the run-up to the Summit of the Future, and the Fourth International Conference on Financing for Development in 2025.

Glossary of key terms

Diet quality (or healthy diets): Comprised of four key aspects: diversity (within and across food groups), adequacy (sufficiency of all essential nutrients compared to requirements), moderation (foods and nutrients that are related to poor health outcomes) and balance (energy and macronutrient intake). Foods consumed should be safe.

Zero Hunger

The global issue of hunger and food insecurity has shown an alarming increase since 2015, a trend exacerbated by a combination of factors including the pandemic, conflict, climate change, and deepening inequalities.

By 2022, approximately 735 million people – or 9.2% of the world's population – found themselves in a state of chronic hunger – a staggering rise compared to 2019. This data underscores the severity of the situation, revealing a growing crisis.

In addition, an estimated 2.4 billion people faced moderate to severe food insecurity in 2022. This classification signifies their lack of access to sufficient nourishment. This number escalated by an alarming 391 million people compared to 2019.

The persistent surge in hunger and food insecurity, fueled by a complex interplay of factors, demands immediate attention and coordinated global efforts to alleviate this critical humanitarian challenge.

Extreme hunger and malnutrition remains a barrier to sustainable development and creates a trap from which people cannot easily escape. Hunger and malnutrition mean less productive individuals, who are more prone to disease and thus often unable to earn more and improve their livelihoods.

Two billion people in the world do not have regular access to safe, nutritious and sufficient food. In 2022, 148 million children had stunted growth and 45 million children under the age of 5 were affected by wasting.

How many people are hungry?

It is projected that more than 600 million people worldwide will be facing hunger in 2030, highlighting the immense challenge of achieving the zero hunger target.

People experiencing moderate food insecurity are typically unable to eat a healthy, balanced diet on a regular basis because of income or other resource constraints.

Why are there so many hungry people?

Shockingly, the world is back at hunger levels not seen since 2005, and food prices remain higher in more countries than in the period

2015–2019. Along with conflict, climate shocks, and rising cost of living, civil insecurity and declining food production have all contributed to food scarcity and high food prices.

Investment in the agriculture sector is critical for reducing hunger and poverty, improving food security, creating employment and building resilience to disasters and shocks.

Why should I care?

We all want our families to have enough food to eat what is safe and nutritious. A world with zero hunger can positively impact our economies, health, education, equality and social development.

It's a key piece of building a better future for everyone. Additionally, with hunger limiting human development, we will not be able to achieve the other sustainable development goals such as education, health and gender equality.

"Goal 2: Zero Hunger" by United Nations.

Food environment: The physical, economic, political and sociocultural context in which consumers engage with agrifood systems to make decisions about acquiring, preparing and consuming food.

Hunger: an uncomfortable or painful sensation caused by insufficient energy from diet. In this report, the term hunger is synonymous with **chronic undernourishment** and is measured by the prevalence of undernourishment (PoU).

Malnutrition: an abnormal physiological condition caused by inadequate, unbalanced or excessive intake of macronutrients and/or micronutrients and/or by disease that causes weight loss. Malnutrition includes undernutrition (child stunting and wasting), vitamin and mineral deficiencies (also known as micronutrient deficiencies) as well as overweight and obesity.

Moderate food insecurity: a level of severity of food insecurity at which people face uncertainties about their ability to obtain food and have been forced to reduce, at times during the year, the quality and/or quantity of food they consume due to lack of money or other resources. It refers to a lack of consistent access to food, which diminishes dietary quality and disrupts normal eating patterns. It is measured with the Food Insecurity Experience Scale and contributes to tracking the progress towards SDG Target 2.1 (Indicator 2.1.2).

Severe food insecurity: a level of severity of food insecurity at which, at some time during the year, people have run out of food, experienced hunger and at the most extreme, gone without food for a day or more. It is measured with the Food Insecurity Experience Scale and contributes to tracking the progress towards SDG Target 2.1 (Indicator 2.1.2).

Undernourishment: a condition in which an individual's habitual food consumption is insufficient to provide the amount of dietary energy required to maintain a normal, active, and healthy life. The prevalence of undernourishment is used to measure hunger and progress towards SDG Target 2.1 (Indicator 2.1.1).

> *"Unfortunately, water scarcity and pollution are becoming more prevalent and affecting poorer populations disproportionately, particularly farmers. Malnutrition levels are also on the rise, particularly in rural areas, and are strongly correlated with water scarcity."*

Water is Crucial to Food Production

Claudia Ringler and Jenna Wilf

In this viewpoint, Claudia Ringler and Jenna Wilf discusses the crucial role of water in food systems and its impact on health, nutrition, and sustainable development, stressing that access to clean water is a basic human right. Claudia Ringler is Deputy Director of the International Food Policy Research Institute's (IFPRI) Environment and Production Technology Division, and Deputy Director of the CGIAR Research Program on Water, Land, and Ecosystems; Jenna Wilf is an IFPRI Project Intern.

As you read, consider the following questions:

1. According to Ringler, how is the supply of water essential for the production of food?
2. According to the viewpoint, how does agriculture dominate the use of water on a global scale?
3. How does Ringler suggest improving water management?

Water is vital for all life and integral to the functioning and productivity of Earth's ecosystems. Water is also central to food systems—as a basic component of food and drink, and in production, processing, and preparation of food. Another use of water, WASH (water supply, sanitation, and hygiene), is essential for human health and nutrition. Access to water and sanitation is a basic human right, like the right to food. Unfortunately, water scarcity and pollution are becoming more prevalent and affecting poorer populations disproportionately, particularly farmers. Malnutrition levels are also on the rise, particularly in rural areas, and are strongly correlated with water scarcity.

Food systems transformation is essential to achieve Sustainable Development Goal 6 on water and sanitation by 2030. Agriculture consumes most the world's freshwater resources—currently, 85% of all freshwater withdrawals are used in agriculture, mostly for the production of cereals, sugarcane, and cotton. Nevertheless, the productivity of such irrigated systems is high—and demand for irrigation continues to grow as a result of growing climate extremes that make rainfed agriculture less resilient. Already today, irrigated crop areas produce 40% of global food on less than a third of global harvested land.

At the same time, food systems cannot be transformed without fully considering water. Around 3 billion people cannot afford a healthy diet, particularly dairy, fruits, vegetables, and protein-rich foods. These cannot be produced without access to sufficient and clean water sources. Climate change, as well as other environmental and societal changes—including land use changes, biodiversity loss, urbanization, and evolving lifestyles and diets—are affecting the dynamics of natural water cycles and water resource availability, with implications for food systems. We must reduce water vulnerabilities to successfully achieve SDG2 on zero hunger and SDG6 on water and sanitation.

Gearing up for the UN Food Systems Summit (UNFSS), a new brief on water and food systems outlines a number of solutions to jointly improve food systems outcomes and water security, including:

Strengthen efforts to preserve water-based ecosystems and their functions. Deforestation and destruction of water-based ecosystems should be stopped, while increasing water supplies, improving water quality, and mitigating risks associated with water-related hazards and climate change. Limits to water consumption should be developed and monitored in water stressed regions.

Improve agricultural water management for better diets for all. Climate change threatens rainfed food systems that produce the bulk of food, fodder, and fiber, as well as animal feed. Investing in more water-efficient crop varieties, improved agronomic practices, better incentives for farmers to conserve upper watersheds, and strong institutions are all key to addressing the threat climate change poses to rainfed food systems. Additionally, irrigation development should be kept in line with environmental limits. There is also huge potential for increasing water and nutrition productivity in irrigation. Finally, addressing water pollution in food production, food safety, and water-based ecosystems is pivotal to improving agricultural water management.

Reduce water and food losses beyond the farm gate. To maximize the benefits of irrigated, perishable high-value crops such as fruits and vegetables, market linkages to consumption centers should be strengthened. This requires investing in physical infrastructure that supports on-farm production, efficient trading and exchange, value addition, and improved transportation and bulk storage.

Coordinate water with nutrition and health interventions. Improving food security, nutrition, and health outcomes, and enhancing women's agency, all depend on better coordination between WASH and irrigation at the government and management levels. To improve positive transmission pathways between these often competing water uses and nutrition and health outcomes, nutrition and health experts must collaborate with water managers at the farm, household, community, and government levels.

Increase the environmental sustainability of food systems. Wide disparities exist between the water footprints of diets in rich and poor countries, and across socioeconomic groups within countries. Food-based dietary recommendations should consider the environmental impact of diets and technologies, and consumer awareness should be improved to reduce food waste and losses.

Address social inequities in water-nutrition linkages. Vulnerable communities must be actively involved in the design and implementation of water systems. Designs should consider multiple uses of water, such as drinking, irrigation, and livestock watering, to meet the needs of rural smallholders who are most vulnerable to both water and food insecurity. With women making up a large share of the agricultural workforce, their productive roles should be promoted, and they should be trained in irrigation and water management.

Improve data quality and monitoring for water-food system linkages, drawing on innovations in information and communications technology (ICT). To fully understand the water footprint of diets and formulate policies that co-maximize water, food security, and nutrition goals, more and better data are needed. This will help to improve water management and food systems, as well as accountability of related policy decisions. This requires long-term investments in global monitoring of a variety of hydrological and food-related parameters.

Water and food security strategies tend to be developed independently from each other, and the UNFSS Food System Summit Action Tracks have no direct focus on water. The seven solutions proposed here, however, can help shape all five tracks or focal areas and thus help to advance both the transformation of our food systems and improve water security for people and the planet.

Periodical and Internet Sources Bibliography

The following articles have been selected to supplement the diverse views presented in this chapter.

Jonathan Foley, "Where Will We Find Enough Food for 9 Billion?" *National Geographic*. https://www.nationalgeographic.com/foodfeatures/feeding-9-billion/.

Liz Goodwin, "The Global Benefits of Reducing Food Loss and Waste, and How to Do It," *Global Resources Institute*, April 20, 2023. https://www.wri.org/insights/reducing-food-loss-and-food-waste.

Michael Grunwald, "Sorry, but This is the Future of Food," *The New York Times*, December 13, 2024. https://www.nytimes.com/2024/12/13/opinion/food-agriculture-factory-farms-climate-change.html.

Matt Hopkins, "The Future of Food Is Zero Waste," The *Atlantic*, January 10, 2020. https://www.theatlantic.com/video/index/604636/zero-waste-silo/.

Sarah Kaplan, "A recipe for fighting climate change and feeding the world," *The Washington Post*, October 12, 2021. https://www.washingtonpost.com/climate-solutions/interactive/2021/bread-baking-sustainable-grain-kernza/.

Sarah Kuta "How will we feed the future and save the planet?" *Johns Hopkins Magazine*, Spring 2023. https://hub.jhu.edu/magazine/2023/spring/feed-the-future-and-save-the-planet/.

Akindare Lewis, "The Global Hunger Crisis: If the World Has Enough Food Why Are People Still Starving?" *Global Citizen*, Aug. 2, 2023. https://www.globalcitizen.org/en/content/hunger-global-citizen-festival-advocacy-food/.

Anahad O'Connor, "Why the best diet for you is also good for the planet," *The Washington Post*, June 10, 2024. https://www.washingtonpost.com/wellness/2024/06/10/planetary-diet-lower-mortality/.

David Wallace-Wells, "Opinion: Food as You Know it is About to Change," *The New York Times*. July 28, 2024. https://www.nytimes.com/2024/07/28/opinion/food-climate-crisis-prices.html.

Chapter 2

What Is the Future of Farming?

Chapter Preface

When Donald J. Trump became president for the second time in January 2025, the Trump administration immediately froze several U.S. Department of Agriculture (USDA) funding programs, sending the U.S. agricultural system into a tizzy. The new administration released a statement defending the new policy, stating that it was their goal to "rein in reckless spending, unleash American energy, cut needless regulations, and make the entire federal government more effective at serving the American people, including our farmers."

For decades, America depended on the family farm to provide sustenance for its population. But as technology and business practices have evolved, the family farm has seen increased competition from corporate farming. The number of American farms has shrunk drastically over the years. Between 2017 and 2024 alone, the number of farms in America fell from 2.04 million to 1.88 million.

But many local farmers claim that competition from corporate farming is not the real enemy. Instead, they assert, ever-increasing government regulation has made it difficult for family farms to turn a profit. When they cannot do so, corporations often swoop in and purchase their farms, as the size and recourses of corporations enable them to deal more effectively with the government.

According to the organization Save Family Farming, there is a solution. They believe that "a critical examination of government policies and regulations [will] ensure they support, rather than hinder, family farms. Streamlining regulatory processes, offering financial support tailored to smaller farms, and ensuring fair competition are essential steps in creating a more equitable and secure agricultural sector."

Wishing for fewer government regulations is a double edged sword for the small farmer. There may be less regulatory impediments going forward, but there also may be less government aid in the form of subsidies and loans when small farms struggle. And who is primed to benefit from the uncertain future? Clearly, corporate mega-farms have more ability to withstand downturns.

The viewpoints in this chapter highlight various paths forward for farmers as they step into the future. From greater support for local farmers to use of the latest technology, you can examine for yourself what you think the future of farming will look like.

Viewpoint 1

> *"For some farmers, the technology's upfront costs are too high, given the potential risk of crop failure due to poor weather."*

Behavioral Science Can Help Optimize Farm Yields

Kaylee Somerville

In this viewpoint, Kaylee Somerville discusses the growing importance of agriculture in response to increasing global food demands, which are projected to rise significantly by 2050 due to a world population of 9.8 billion. Somerville believes that behavioral science could play a role in overcoming these barriers and improving the implementation of agtech solutions among farmers. Kaylee Somerville is a research and teaching assistant at the University of Calgary in the areas of finance, entrepreneurship, and workplace harassment.

As you read, consider the following questions:

1. According to Somerville, how does precision agriculture improve crop yields?
2. Similarly, what are the positive effects of using AI and automation in agriculture?
3. According to Somerville, why are many Canadian farmers not taking advantage of new technologies?

"Behavioral Science and the Future of Agriculture" by Kaylee Somerville, *The Decision Lab*, Noveember 30, 2020. Reprinted by permission.

While sectors in different areas are diminishing, one industry that will continue to grow is agriculture. We all need to eat, and the demands on agriculture are increasing at a steady pace. A global population of 9.8 billion is predicted by 2050, and experts predict overall food demand and animal-based food demand to increase by more than 50 percent and 70 percent, respectively.[1,2]

Canada is specifically impacted by this demand, being one of the world's largest agricultural exporters. The Canadian government has set its sights on growing its agri-food exports to at least $75 billion annually by 2025.[3] While the demand for food increases, so does the need for sustainable practices, as agriculture and related land-use change generate one quarter of annual greenhouse gas (GHG) emissions.[2]

Solutions are being developed to help solve these problems. The agriculture technology industry, abbreviated as "agtech," is becoming more populated and diverse. Experts believe agtech will become a $730 billion (USD) industry worldwide by 2023,[17] and Canada is not behind in contributing to the startup sector. The Vancouver-based Terramera believes their pest control technology could reduce synthetic pesticides by 80% and increase crop yields by 20% globally.[4] Decisive Farming, an agtech startup headquartered in Irricana, Alberta, offers a platform that streamlines farming processes and optimizes production. And Calgary's Verge Ag uses land data and artificial intelligence to create specialized GPS paths that machinery can follow to work on behalf of farmers.[5] These technologies, and others, have the potential to revolutionize the agriculture industry.

Despite the promise of agtech, the adoption of many of these new tools has been slow. Behavioral science might offer a solution to this problem, shining a light on the reasons why some technologies haven't caught on and providing interventions to fix that.

Before talking about the role of behavioral science in agriculture, though, let's take a look at two significant categories in agtech: Precision agriculture, and automation and artificial intelligence

Understanding the Future of Agriculture

Agriculture is the lifeblood of human civilization, responsible for feeding a global population that is expected to reach nearly 10 billion by 2050.

This growth, coupled with rapid urbanization, presents both an incredible opportunity and a looming challenge. As more people move into cities, the distance between food production and consumption grows, placing unprecedented pressure on supply chains. In this context, the agricultural industry is not only vital for feeding the world but also has a profound impact on economic stability, social equity, and environmental sustainability.

The future of agriculture will be shaped by a vast array of market forces. Futureworld has taken a view on five powerful forces that will drive innovation, disrupt traditional business models, and redefine the journey from farm to fork:

Technological Innovation: Efficiency at Scale
Climate Change Adaptation: Resilience in the Face of Crisis
Regenerative Agriculture: Meeting Demand for Responsible Farming
Shifting Consumer Preferences: The Demand for Local and Healthy Foods
Geopolitics: Ensuring Food Security in a Complex World

"Understanding the Future of Agriculture" by futureworld.org, October 22, 2024.

Precision agriculture

Precision agriculture uses remote sensors to analyze the needs of individuals crops. Because each crop and field is different, the technology allows for precise information to maximize yield per crop. With this technology, farmers can be selective in their resource use and only deploy resources like water and fertilizer in locations where they're needed.[3] Precision technology also improves dairy and livestock farming, with sensor systems that measure animal behavior and health, helping farmers' decision-making.[6]

Overall, precision agriculture is an incredibly helpful tool for decision-making optimization. This technology has several key benefits: reducing resource costs for farmers, reducing the risk of over-fertilization, and improving sustainability.[6,7]

Artificial intelligence, automation, and agriculture

Technological advances allow for autonomous vehicles and equipment to be employed in fields 24/7, increasing productivity, reducing food waste, and protecting farmers' safety. One example of AI technology in the agriculture industry is facial recognition software for cows, which provides farmers with the ability to track individual animals' health in detailed ways. Other uses of AI include using data to decide where to apply which type of herbicide, and predicting upcoming weather patterns to help farmers in their decision-making.[18]

However, the uptake of these technologies is low.6 Researchers found that in Germany, only 10–30% of farmers use new tools such as these.[19]

Why aren't farmers using agtech?

A regularly discussed setback is the cost of new technologies. For some farmers, the technology's upfront costs are too high, given the potential risk of crop failure due to poor weather. The variability of crop prices year by year can also make farmers more careful with their capital investment.[1,9]

Additionally, many emerging technologies involve the use and integration of data across different products. Evan Fraser, a professor at the University of Guelph who researches farmer behavior, states that data interoperability, data governance, and cybersecurity are the most significant challenges for farmers adopting the technology. Ransomware hacks are threatening in any context, but could be devastating for farmers; Dr. Fraser provides the potential scenario of cyber hackers remotely taking control of a poultry farm ventilator, which would have drastic consequences for the farm.[10]

Both cost- and data-related factors are contributors to the slow adoption of agtech, with due cause. These challenges considerably impact adoption and will need to be solved through technological improvements to decrease the cost while improving security.

But behavioral science can also help speed up agtech's adoption, and policy makers should start to consider its use. Luckily, research is increasing in this sector, showing effective behavioral interventions that improve technology adoption.

> *"It is time to think about biodiversity as part of the policy package and not just blindly increase productivity."*

Agricultural Subsidies Must Change With the Times

Ashok Gulati

In this viewpoint, Ashok Gulati discusses the need to reform agricultural subsidies, particularly in India, to address their negative impact on biodiversity and the environment. Gulati notes that current subsidies, which amount to nearly fifty billion dollars, primarily support staple crops like rice and wheat, leading to monocultures and habitat degradation. He emphasizes the importance of transitioning to "smart subsidies" that promote sustainable farming practices aligned with biodiversity conservation. Gulati believes that financial incentives should be provided to farmers who adopt environmentally friendly methods. Ashok Gulati is an Indian agricultural economist and a former chairman of the Commission for Agricultural Costs and Prices (CACP), the advisory body of the Government of India on food supplies and pricing policies.

"Repurposing agricultural subsidies for the benefit of farmers and nature," by Dr. Ashok Gulati, BIOFIN, April 30, 2024. Reprinted by permission.

As you read, consider the following questions:

1. What changes in the food supply have caused Gulati to reconsider farming subsidies?
2. According to Gulati, how do current subsidies impede biodiversity?
3. What new policy innovations does Gulati suggest?

Excerpts from the presentation by Dr. Ashok Gulati at the 10th BIOFIN East Asia Pacific Regional Dialogue

Transcribed and prepared by Abbie Trinidad, Senior Technical Advisor, UNDP BIOFIN Global and Ainur Shalakhanova, Environment Finance Analyst, UNDP BIOFIN Global

Target 18 of the Global Biodiversity Framework recognizes the environmental and financial impacts of the continued use of subsidies and therefore aims to progressively reduce funding by at least US$ 500 billion per year by 2030. According to OECD estimates, this amount supports agricultural production in 54 countries, leading to habitat destruction, soil degradation and nutrient pollution. Repurposing this ineffective and unsustainable support could lead to significant fiscal savings and free up scarce resources to contribute to the other SDGs.

Currently, BIOFIN is working in 27 countries to analyse the harmful effects of subsidies on biodiversity and create action plans to rethink and redesign them. In India, BIOFIN is fortunate to benefit from the experience and wisdom of eminent scientist Dr Ashok Gulati. Dr Ashok attended the EAPAC Regional Dialogue in Sigiriya in November 2023 and shared his insights on the topic of repurposing harmful subsidies. This article is an excerpt from Dr Gulati's presentation.

Agriculture subsidies in India and globally

All over the world, most countries—even the G20 countries subsidize their agriculture. There are various policy instruments that are used to subsidise. In developed countries, prices are generally higher than they would be with free trade. So, there is protection in the form of output prices.

However, some developing countries subsidise inputs because they want to maintain low inputs and low output prices. There is a reason for this—even for large countries like India, China or Indonesia, which have large populations to feed. The first and most important task of any government is to ensure the food security of its people. The Green Revolution introduced high-yielding varieties and prevented famines. However, it was also supported by subsidising primary inputs such as fertilisers.

These subsidies were introduced in India in the 1970s and have expanded to around US$ 24 billion to date. Then there is another food subsidy for consumers, especially for wheat and rice. India gives five kilogrammes of wheat and rice per person free of cost to more than 800 million people every month through the Prime Minister's Garib Kalyan Yojana. This is perhaps the largest food security programme in the world. In total, these two subsidies, fertiliser and food subsidies in India, amount to nearly US$48-49 billion. However, output prices are controlled, and input prices are subsidized.

The bottom line is that the OECD has made an estimate of the so-called producer subsidies. According to this, India has a negative estimate of producer subsidies. Most developed countries, all OECD countries, have a subsidy of 14% to 15% on both the input and output side. But India subsidizes its inputs but also suppresses the output prices, which is called market price support, and that is negative, while the budget subsidy through inputs is positive. So the bottom line is that Indian farmers are implicitly taxed and not subsidised. However, this does not mean that inputs are not subsidised. Fertilisers are very heavily subsidised, which has an impact on biodiversity.

Observations from India on mapping harmful subsidies

Fertilizer subsidies promote and increase the production of staple crops: rice, wheat and sugarcane. This support has led to monocultures because farmers make high profits from

Arguments for and Against Farm Subsidies in Developing Countries

Here is a brief synopsis of some of the arguments for and against farm subsidies in developing countries

Historically, countries with large agricultural sectors and less developed economies tend to have a higher percentage of GDP coming from farming.

For example, in sub-Saharan Africa, many countries have over 30% of their GDP coming from agriculture. In some countries, such as Malawi, Burkina Faso, and Sierra Leone, the figure is over 50%. Similarly, in Asia, countries like Nepal and Laos have a large share of GDP coming from agriculture. In the Americas, Haiti is one example of a country where farming represents a high percentage of GDP.

Farm subsidies in developing countries are a contentious issue, with arguments for and against their use.

Arguments in favour of farm subsidies include:

- Improving food security: Subsidies can help smallholder farmers increase their production, which can improve food security for the country.
- Higher per capita incomes can reduce extreme poverty in rural areas and prevent high levels of rural - urban migration
- Encouraging sustainable farming practices: Subsidies can be used to encourage farmers to adopt environmentally-friendly practices, such as reducing the use of pesticides and fertilizers.

crops such as rice, while competing crops such as oilseeds, pulses or millets require less fertiliser. These may be more nutritious, but since there are subsidies and rice is the staple crop in most Asian countries, at least in South and South East Asian countries, especially India, and people are committed

- Supporting farmers facing economic difficulties: Subsidies can help farmers facing economic difficulties as a result of market fluctuations or changes in government policies.

Arguments against farm subsidies include:

- Distorting markets: Subsidies can artificially lower the price of agricultural products, making it difficult for farmers in other countries to compete. This can be seen as a form of trade protectionism.
- Encouraging overproduction: Subsidies can lead to overproduction, which can then result in surplus and lower prices, which in turn might hurt farmers incomes.
- Over-production can lead to negative externalities from production which threatens sustainable growth and development
- Limited public resources: Subsidies can be a significant expense for the government in a developing country, and may then divert fiscal resources away from other important public services such as access to basic education, health care and infrastructure.
- Limited to certain farmers: Subsidies can be targeted to certain farmers, such as large-scale producers, leaving small farmers with fewer resources. In many lower-income countries, small-holder farms are unable to fully reap the benefits of government subsidy.

"Arguments for and against farm subsidies in developing countries" by Tutor2u.

to growing rice and wheat, this is the rotation. In some states like Punjab, the seat of the green revolution, a monoculture has developed where the success of one variety crowds out all others, which in turn has a negative impact on the biodiversity of the region.

SWAB: a smart approach to redesigning harmful subsidies

When the subsidy programme was designed and implemented, extreme poverty in India was over 60% and political philosophy dictated measures such as low input and output prices. Today, extreme poverty in India as defined by the World Bank at $2.15 PPP is around 11%. There is not much sign of extreme poverty anymore and it is time to let market forces work.

Part of this transition is to support farmers in a smart way: smart subsidies. Smart subsidies focus on agricultural practises that are in harmony with nature, i.e. protecting biodiversity, protecting soil, protecting water and minimising greenhouse gas emissions. You could call it SWAB: Soil, Water, Air and Biodiversity as a holistic package, and farmers who opt for such practises must be rewarded for doing so.

This is where the new policy innovation is needed, where farmers who adopt good practises and take all these things into account get additional credits—green credits, biodiversity credits, carbon credits, greenhouse gas emissions and climate resilience. Financial products and policies are needed that can incentivise farmers to promote biodiversity.

Raising awareness as a first step towards redesigning harmful subsidies

Policy is embedded in a political economy framework. First, policy makers need to recognise that the context in which these policies were created has changed, that the background has changed and that this should also apply to the policy. Poverty has declined and there is no longer a shortage of staple foods in India as there was in the 1960s or 70s.

Since the supply of food is sufficient, market forces must prevail because there is no longer any reason for subsidies. For example, the prices of fertilisers such as urea are subsidized by 85% to 90%, which has led to abuse or oversupply. However, the plant only absorbs 35% to 40% of the nitrogen. The rest is released into the environment as nitrous oxide or leaches into the water and damages water bodies. This is a story where the success of one variety of wheat or rice causes it to spread over millions of hectares but harms the concept of biodiversity.

One way to solve this problem is to grow many other crops on the same platform. For example, millet, pulses or oilseeds that fix nitrogen. These crops are not as heavily subsidised with nitrogen, nor are they as heavily subsidised as the $24 billion. As such, they are better for nature and biodiversity and also more economical. Policies that give equal treatment or fair treatment, in fact, better treatment to those that promote biodiversity should be designed.

This is certainly a sensitive issue. It needs to be discussed with farmers and priorities need to be communicated to farmers in a timely manner. It is time to think about nature. It is time to think about biodiversity as part of the policy package and not just blindly increase productivity.

Making agricultural practices more conducive to biodiversity conservation

A calibrated "carrot and stick" formula is needed. People cannot be forced, so the "stick" needs to be minimised, while the "carrot" needs to be increased to incentivise farmers. Farmers will adopt the new practises through constant education. They also look at their profitability. They may want to protect biodiversity, but if their profit drops by 20%, they are unlikely to adopt any of the practises we are asking for.

So, the whole system needs to be changed to get smart subsidies that are consistent with the promotion of biodiversity. The profitability of the farmer and the farmer must take centre stage and he will be guided by the profits of the crops he grows. If these profits can be realigned in a way that promotes biodiversity, then we can hope for a success story. Otherwise, it is a losing battle.

"Locally sourced produce simply tastes better. When food is grown nearby and picked at the peak of ripeness, it retains more of its natural sweetness and flavor."

Locally Sourced Produce Is Beneficial to All of Us

Ruth Linton

In this viewpoint, Ruth Linton highlights the importance of small farms, focusing on their role in supporting local food systems, enhancing community relationships, and providing fresher, more flavorful food. She also discusses the farm-to-table movement, which aims to connect consumers with local producers and promote sustainable farming practices. Ruth Linton shares her knowledge of farming through courses, books, social media, and in-person talks. She grew up on a Delaware farm, earned her M.A. in History from the University of Delaware, worked and lived in various parts of the United States, and has run her own family farm since 1996.

"Small Farms, Big Flavors: Exploring the Benefits of Locally Sourced Produce" by Ruth, Highland Orchards, April 3, 2024. Reprinted by permission.

As you read, consider the following questions:

1. According to Linton, why is locally sourced food superior to that of factory farms?
2. According to Linton, how should consumers go about finding locally sourced food?
3. How could the farm-to-table movement continue to inspire the future of food?

Small farms are more than just picturesque scenery on the outskirts of town. They are the backbone of our local food systems, providing fresh, healthy produce that is packed with flavor and nutrients. In recent years, there has been a growing interest in locally sourced food, and for good reason. From reducing the environmental impact of food transportation to supporting local economies, buying from small farms has numerous benefits. But perhaps the biggest advantage of all is the taste. Locally sourced produce simply tastes better. When food is grown nearby and picked at the peak of ripeness, it retains more of its natural sweetness and flavor. In this article, we'll explore the benefits of small farms and locally sourced produce, and why it's worth seeking out these gems at your local farmer's market or grocery store.

What Makes Locally Sourced Produce Different?

Locally sourced produce is different from conventionally grown produce in several ways. The first difference is the way it is grown. Small farms tend to use more sustainable farming practices that focus on soil health and biodiversity. They rely less on synthetic fertilizers and pesticides and more on composting, cover crops, crop rotation, and the use of natural predators to control pests. This means that the produce is grown in a healthier, more natural environment, resulting in healthier, more flavorful fruits and vegetables.

Another difference is the way the produce is handled after it is harvested. Small farms don't have to worry about shipping their produce long distances or storing it for long periods of time. This means that the produce can be picked at the peak of ripeness and delivered to local markets within hours of being harvested. This results in produce that is fresher, tastier, and more nutrient-dense.

Finally, there is the social aspect of buying locally sourced produce. When you buy from a small farm, you are not only supporting the local economy, but you are also building a relationship with the farmer who grew your food. This creates a sense of community and trust that is often lacking in our modern food system.

Benefits of Eating Locally Sourced Produce

The benefits of eating locally sourced produce are numerous. Here are 4 top benefits:

Health Benefits

Locally sourced produce is often fresher and more nutrient-dense than conventionally grown produce. Because it is picked at the peak of ripeness and delivered to local markets quickly, it retains more of its natural vitamins and minerals. It is also less likely to be contaminated with harmful pesticides or bacteria, making it safer to eat.

Environmental Benefits

Transporting food long distances requires a lot of energy and produces a lot of greenhouse gas emissions. When you buy locally sourced produce, you are reducing the carbon footprint of your food. You are also supporting small farms that use more sustainable farming practices, which helps to protect the environment.

Economic Benefits

Buying from small farms supports the local economy by keeping money in the community. It also helps to create jobs and preserve farmland, which is becoming increasingly rare in many parts of the country.

Taste Benefits

Perhaps the most obvious benefit of eating locally sourced produce is the taste. When produce is grown nearby and picked at the peak of ripeness, it simply tastes better. It is sweeter, juicier, and more flavorful than produce that has been shipped long distances or stored for long periods of time.

Understanding the Farm-to-Table Movement

The farm-to-table movement is a growing trend in the food industry that emphasizes the importance of locally sourced, sustainable food. It seeks to connect consumers with local farmers and food producers, and to create a more transparent, sustainable food system.

One of the main goals of the farm-to-table movement is to reduce the distance between where food is grown and where it is consumed. This helps to reduce the environmental impact of food transportation and to support local farmers. It also helps to create a closer relationship between consumers and the food they eat, which can lead to a greater appreciation for the work that goes into producing our food.

Another goal of the farm-to-table movement is to promote sustainable farming practices. This includes using cover crops, composting, crop rotation, and other techniques that help to build healthy soil and reduce the use of synthetic fertilizers and pesticides. By supporting small farms that use these practices, consumers can help to protect the environment and promote more sustainable agriculture.

The Impact of Locally Sourced Produce on the Environment

Buying locally sourced produce has a number of environmental benefits. One of the most significant is the reduction in greenhouse gas emissions. When food is transported long distances, it requires a lot of energy and produces a lot of carbon emissions. By buying locally sourced produce, you are reducing the carbon footprint of your food.

Another environmental benefit of locally sourced produce is the promotion of sustainable farming practices. Small farms tend to use more sustainable techniques that focus on soil health and biodiversity. This helps to protect the environment by reducing the use of synthetic fertilizers and pesticides and promoting the use of natural predators to control pests.

Finally, buying locally sourced produce helps to preserve farmland and support local ecosystems. When small farms are able to stay in business, they are more likely to preserve their land as open space. This can help to protect local wildlife and promote biodiversity.

Supporting Local Farmers and the Local Economy

Buying locally sourced produce is a great way to support local farmers and the local economy. When you buy from a small farm, you are keeping money in the community and supporting local jobs. You are also helping to preserve farmland and promote sustainable agriculture.

Another way to support local farmers is to join a CSA (Community Supported Agriculture) program. These programs allow consumers to buy a share of a local farm's produce and receive a weekly or bi-weekly box of fresh, seasonal produce. This helps to support the farmer by providing a consistent source of income, and it also allows consumers to try a variety of produce that they may not have otherwise tried.

How to Find Locally Sourced Produce Near You

Finding locally sourced produce near you is easier than you might think. Here are a four tips that can take you to your new favorite farm:

Visit Your Local Farmer's Market

One of the best ways to find locally sourced produce is to visit your local farmer's market. These markets bring together local farmers and food producers, allowing consumers to buy fresh, seasonal produce directly from the source. Farmer's markets are also a great way to build connections with local farmers and learn more about where your food comes from.

Join a CSA Program

As mentioned earlier, joining a CSA program is a great way to support local farmers and receive a regular supply of fresh, seasonal produce. Many CSA programs also offer farm tours and other events that allow consumers to connect with the farmer and learn more about sustainable agriculture.

Check Your Local Grocery Store

Some grocery stores or specialty markets now carry locally sourced produce. Look for signs or labels that indicate where the produce was grown. You can also ask the store manager or produce manager if they carry locally sourced produce.

Visit Local Farms

Some small farms allow visitors to come and pick their own produce. This is a fun way to get out in nature and support local farmers at the same time. Other farms have an on-farm market, so you can get your produce directly from the farm. Check with local farms to see if they offer this option.

Tips for Cooking with Locally Sourced Produce

Cooking with locally sourced produce can be a fun and rewarding experience. Here are a four tips to help you get the most out of your local produce:

Keep it Simple

When you have fresh, flavorful produce, you don't need a lot of fancy ingredients to make it taste good. Keep your recipes simple and let the natural flavors of the produce shine through.

Experiment with New Flavors

Locally sourced produce often includes a variety of unique and unusual flavors. Don't be afraid to try something new and experiment with different flavor combinations. Fresh herbs are a great way to add zest to your meal, and your local farm most likely has your favorite herbs.

Use What's in Season

Locally sourced produce is often only available during certain times of the year. Take advantage of this by using what's in season and experimenting with different recipes that highlight the flavors of the season. What is in season has the best flavor!

Preserve Excess Produce

If you have excess produce, consider preserving it for later use. This can include canning, freezing, or dehydrating the produce. This allows you to enjoy the flavors of locally sourced produce even when it's out of season.

Incorporating Locally Sourced Produce into Your Daily Diet

Incorporating locally sourced produce into your daily diet is easy and fun. Here are a few ideas to help you get started:

Start Small

Don't feel overwhelmed by the idea of completely changing your diet. Start small by incorporating one or two locally sourced produce items into your meals each week.

Shop at the Farmer's Market

As mentioned earlier, shopping at the farmer's market is a great way to find locally sourced produce. Make it a habit to visit the market at least once a week and try something new each time. If you can make it part of your routine, then you build a good habit of eating fresh produce. In addition, by shopping at the farm regularly, you will not miss any of your favorite foods that may have a short season, such as strawberries.

Join a CSA Program

Joining a CSA program can help you incorporate locally sourced produce into your diet on a regular basis. You'll receive a box of fresh, seasonal produce each week or every other week, which will help you to try new things and experiment with different recipes. This way you do not have to decide what is in season or not; the farmer knows and you get the benefits!

Grow Your Own Produce

If you have space, consider starting a small garden and growing your own produce. This will allow you to enjoy the flavors of locally sourced produce right in your own backyard. Your local farm may have exactly what you are looking for in the spring for young plants to get your garden growing.

Conclusion

Locally sourced produce is more than just a trendy buzzword. It is a way to support local farmers, promote sustainable agriculture, and enjoy fresh, flavorful produce that is packed with nutrients. Whether you shop at the farmer's market, join a CSA program, or grow your own produce, there are many ways to incorporate locally sourced produce into your daily diet. So next time you're at the grocery store or farmer's market, take a closer look at where your food comes from and consider buying locally sourced produce. Your taste buds, your health, and your community will thank you.

If you are close to Wilmington, Delaware, we invite you to come visit our farm and farm market here at Highland Orchards. If not, please find a farm near you to support; www.LocalHarvest.org is an excellent source for finding a farm nearby.

Happy eating!

Viewpoint 4

> *"Past advances were mostly mechanical, in the form of more powerful and efficient machinery, and genetic, in the form of more productive seed and fertilizers. Now much more sophisticated, digital tools are needed to deliver the next productivity leap."*

Digital Technology is Integral to the Future of Food

Lutz Goedde, Joshua Katz, Alexandre Ménard, and Julien Revellat

In this viewpoint, the authors discuss the significant transformation of the agriculture industry over the past 50 years, focusing on the role of advanced technologies such as artificial intelligence, data analytics, and connectivity in enhancing productivity and sustainability. They stress the necessity of creating a robust connectivity infrastructure that will unlock an estimated $500 billion in additional value to the global economy by 2030, driven by the growing demand for food despite limitations in land and resources. Joshua Katz, Alexandre Ménard, and Julien Revellat work at McKinsey & Company, a global management consulting firm founded in 1926. The firm advises companies and organizations on strategy, operations, and other business challenges to improve their performance and growth. Katz is a Partner, who works out of Darien, Connecticut. Ménard is a

"Agriculture's connected future: How technology can yield new growth" McKinsey. October 9, 2020. Reprinted by permission.

Senior Partner who coleads the Industry and Technology Practice in France. Revellat serves clients in the agriculture and agri-food industry in France, Europe, the Middle East, and Africa. Lutz Goedde is a Partner at Paine Schwartz Partners, a private equity firm specializing in sustainable food chain investing.

As you read, consider the following questions:

1. According to the viewpoint, why is harnessing new digital technology so vital to the future of food?
2. According to the authors, how did the COVID-19 pandemic affect farming worldwide?
3. A corporation such as McKinsey & Company clearly has a monetary stake in improving the production of food. How does the viewpoint reflect that interest?

The agriculture industry has radically transformed over the past 50 years. Advances in machinery have expanded the scale, speed, and productivity of farm equipment, leading to more efficient cultivation of more land. Seed, irrigation, and fertilizers also have vastly improved, helping farmers increase yields. Now, agriculture is in the early days of yet another revolution, at the heart of which lie data and connectivity. Artificial intelligence, analytics, connected sensors, and other emerging technologies could further increase yields, improve the efficiency of water and other inputs, and build sustainability and resilience across crop cultivation and animal husbandry.

The future of connectivity

Without a solid connectivity infrastructure, however, none of this is possible. If connectivity is implemented successfully in agriculture, the industry could tack on $500 billion in additional value to the global gross domestic product by 2030, according to our research. This would amount to a 7 to 9 percent improvement from its expected total and would alleviate much of the present pressure on farmers. It is one of just seven sectors that, fueled by advanced connectivity, will contribute $2 trillion to $3 trillion in additional value to global GDP over the next decade, according to research by the McKinsey Center for Advanced Connectivity and the McKinsey Global Institute (MGI)

Insights to Impact

Demand for food is growing at the same time the supply side faces constraints in land and farming inputs. The world's population is on track to reach 9.7 billion by 2050, requiring a corresponding 70 percent increase in calories available for consumption, even as the cost of the inputs needed to generate those calories is rising. By 2030, the water supply will fall 40 percent short of meeting global water needs, and rising energy, labor, and nutrient costs are already pressuring profit margins. About one-quarter of arable land is degraded and needs significant restoration before it can again sustain crops at scale. And then there are increasing environmental pressures, such as climate change and the economic impact of catastrophic weather events, and social pressures, including the push for more ethical and sustainable farm practices, such as higher standards for farm-animal welfare and reduced use of chemicals and water.

To address these forces poised to further roil the industry, agriculture must embrace a digital transformation enabled by connectivity. Yet agriculture remains less digitized compared with many other industries globally. Past advances were mostly mechanical, in the form of more powerful and efficient machinery, and genetic, in the form of more productive seed and fertilizers. Now much more sophisticated, digital tools are needed to deliver the next productivity leap. Some already exist to help farmers more efficiently and sustainably use resources, while more advanced ones are in development. These new technologies can upgrade decision making, allowing better risk and variability management to optimize yields and improve economics. Deployed in animal husbandry, they can enhance the well-being of livestock, addressing the growing concerns over animal welfare.

Demand for food is growing at the same time the supply side faces constraints in land and farming inputs.

But the industry confronts two significant obstacles. Some regions lack the necessary connectivity infrastructure, making development of it paramount. In regions that already have a connectivity infrastructure, farms have been slow to deploy digital tools because their impact has not been sufficiently proven.

Most Popular Insights

- One year of agentic AI: Six lessons from the people doing the work
- McKinsey Technology Trends Outlook 2025
- The state of AI: How organizations are rewiring to capture value
- The infrastructure moment
- The economic potential of generative AI: The next productivity frontier

The COVID-19 crisis has further intensified other challenges agriculture faces in five areas: efficiency, resilience, digitization, agility, and sustainability. Lower sales volumes have pressured margins, exacerbating the need for farmers to contain costs further. Gridlocked global supply chains have highlighted the importance of having more local providers, which could increase the resilience of smaller farms. In this global pandemic, heavy reliance on manual labor has further affected farms whose workforces face mobility restrictions. Additionally, significant environmental benefits from decreased travel and consumption during the crisis are likely to drive a desire for more local, sustainable sourcing, requiring producers to adjust long-standing practices. In short, the crisis has accentuated the necessity of more widespread digitization and automation, while suddenly shifting demand and sales channels have underscored the value of agile adaptation.

Current connectivity in agriculture

In recent years, many farmers have begun to consult data about essential variables like soil, crops, livestock, and weather. Yet few if any have had access to advanced digital tools that would help to turn these data into valuable, actionable insights. In less-developed regions, almost all farmwork is manual, involving little or no advanced connectivity or equipment.

Even in the United States, a pioneer country in connectivity, only about one-quarter of farms currently use any connected equipment or devices to access data, and that technology isn't exactly state-of-the-art, running on 2G or 3G networks that telcos plan to dismantle or on very low-band IoT networks that are complicated and expensive to set up. In either case, those networks can support only a limited number of devices and lack the performance for real-time data transfer, which is essential to unlock the value of more advanced and complex use cases.

Nonetheless, current IoT technologies running on 3G and 4G cellular networks are in many cases sufficient to enable simpler use cases, such as advanced monitoring of crops and livestock. In the past, however, the cost of hardware was high, so the business case for implementing IoT in farming did not hold up. Today, device and hardware costs are dropping rapidly, and several providers now offer solutions at a price we believe will deliver a return in the first year of investment.

These simpler tools are not enough, though, to unlock all the potential value that connectivity holds for agriculture. To attain that, the industry must make full use of digital applications and analytics, which will require low latency, high bandwidth, high resiliency, and support for a density of devices offered by advanced and frontier connectivity technologies like LPWAN, 5G, and LEO satellites (Exhibit 1).

Exhibit 1

Over the next decade, existing connectivity technologies will advance and totally new ones will emerge.

The challenge the industry is facing is thus twofold: infrastructure must be developed to enable the use of connectivity in farming, and where connectivity already exists, strong business cases must be made in order for solutions to be adopted. The good news is that connectivity coverage is increasing almost everywhere. By 2030, we expect advanced connectivity infrastructure of some type to cover roughly 80 percent of the world's rural areas; the notable exception is Africa, where only a quarter of its area will be covered. The key, then, is to develop more—and more effective—digital tools for the industry and to foster widespread adoption of them.

As connectivity increasingly takes hold, these tools will enable new capabilities in agriculture:

- Massive Internet of Things. Low-power networks and cheaper sensors will set the stage for the IoT to scale up, enabling such use cases as precision irrigation of field crops, monitoring of large herds of livestock, and tracking of the use and performance of remote buildings and large fleets of machinery.
- Mission-critical services. Ultralow latency and improved stability of connections will foster confidence to run applications that demand absolute reliability and responsiveness, such as operating autonomous machinery and drones.
- Near-global coverage. If LEO satellites attain their potential, they will enable even the most remote rural areas of the world to use extensive digitization, which will enhance global farming productivity.

Connectivity's potential for value creation

By the end of the decade, enhanced connectivity in agriculture could add more than $500 billion to global gross domestic product, a critical productivity improvement of 7 to 9 percent for the industry. Much of that value, however, will require investments in connectivity that today are largely absent from agriculture. Other industries already use technologies like LPWAN, cloud computing, and cheaper, better sensors requiring minimal hardware, which can significantly reduce the necessary investment. We have analyzed five use cases—crop monitoring, livestock monitoring, building and equipment management, drone farming, and autonomous farming machinery—where enhanced connectivity is already in the early stages of being used and is most likely to deliver the higher yields, lower costs, and greater resilience and sustainability that the industry needs to thrive in the 21st century.

It's important to note that use cases do not apply equally across regions. For example, in North America, where yields are already fairly optimized, monitoring solutions do not have the same potential for value creation as in Asia or Africa, where there is much more room to improve productivity. Drones and autonomous machinery will deliver more impact to advanced markets, as technology will likely be more readily available there

About the use-case research

Potential value initially will accrue to large farms that have more investing power and better incentives to digitize. Connectivity promises easier surveying of large tracts, and the fixed costs of developing IoT solutions are more easily offset in large production facilities than on small family farms. Crops like cereals, grains, fruits, and vegetables will generate most of the value we identified, for similar reasons. Connectivity enables more use cases in these sectors than in meat and dairy, because of the large average size of farms, relatively higher player consolidation, and better applicability of connected technologies, as IoT networks are especially adapted to static monitoring of many variables. It's also interesting to note that Asia should garner about 60 percent of the total value simply because it produces the biggest volume of crops.

Use case 1: Crop monitoring

Connectivity offers a variety of ways to improve the observation and care of crops. Integrating weather data, irrigation, nutrient, and other systems could improve resource use and boost yields by more accurately identifying and predicting deficiencies. For instance, sensors deployed to monitor soil conditions could communicate via LPWAN, directing sprinklers to adjust water and nutrient application. Sensors could also deliver imagery from remote corners of fields to assist farmers in making more informed and timely decisions and getting early warnings of problems like disease or pests.

Smart monitoring could also help farmers optimize the harvesting window. Monitoring crops for quality characteristics—say, sugar content and fruit color—could help farmers maximize the revenue from their crops.

Most IoT networks today cannot support imagery transfer between devices, let alone autonomous imagery analysis, nor can they support high enough device numbers and density to monitor large fields accurately. Narrowband Internet of Things (NB-IoT) and 5G promise to solve these bandwidth and connection-density issues. The use of more and smoother connections between soil, farm equipment, and farm managers could unlock $130 billion to $175 billion in value by 2030.

Use case 2: Livestock monitoring

Preventing disease outbreaks and spotting animals in distress are critical in large-scale livestock management, where most animals are raised in close quarters on a regimen that ensures they move easily through a highly automated processing system. Chips and body sensors that measure temperature, pulse, and blood pressure, among other indicators, could detect illnesses early, preventing herd infection and improving food quality. Farmers are already using ear-tag technology from providers such as Smartbow (part of Zoetis) to monitor cows' heat, health, and location, or technology from companies such as Allflex to implement comprehensive electronic tracing in case of disease outbreaks.

Similarly, environmental sensors could trigger automatic adjustments in ventilation or heating in barns, lessening distress and improving living conditions that increasingly concern consumers. Better monitoring of animal health and growth conditions could produce $70 billion to $90 billion in value by 2030.

Use case 3: Building and equipment management

Chips and sensors to monitor and measure levels of silos and warehouses could trigger automated reordering, reducing inventory costs for farmers, many of whom are already using such systems from companies like Blue Level Technologies. Similar tools could also improve shelf life of inputs and reduce post-harvest losses by monitoring and automatically optimizing storage conditions. Monitoring conditions and usage of buildings and equipment also has the potential to reduce energy consumption. Computer vision and sensors attached to equipment and connected to predictive-maintenance systems could decrease repair costs and extend machinery and equipment life.

Such solutions could achieve $40 billion to $60 billion in cost savings by 2030.

Use case 4: Farming by drone

Agriculture has been using drones for some two decades, with farmers around the world relying on pioneers like Yamaha's RMAX remote-controlled helicopter to help with crop spraying. Now the next generation of drones is starting to impact the sector, with the ability to survey crops and herds over vast areas quickly and efficiently or as a relay system for ferrying real-time data to other connected equipment and installations. Drones also could use computer vision to analyze field conditions and deliver precise interventions like fertilizers, nutrients, and pesticides where crops most need them. Or they could plant seed in remote locations, lowering equipment and workforce costs. By reducing costs and improving yields, the use of drones could generate between $85 billion and $115 billion in value.

Use case 5: Autonomous farming machinery

More precise GPS controls paired with computer vision and sensors could advance the deployment of smart and autonomous farm machinery. Farmers could operate a variety of equipment on their field simultaneously and without human intervention, freeing up time and other resources. Autonomous machines are also more efficient and precise at working a field than human-operated ones, which could generate fuel savings and higher yields. Increasing the autonomy of machinery through better connectivity could create $50 billion to $60 billion of additional value by 2030.

Additional sources of value

Connected technologies offer an additional, indirect benefit, the value of which is not included in the estimates given in these use cases. The global farming industry is highly fragmented, with most labor done by individual farm owners. Particularly in Asia and Africa, few farms employ outside workers. On such farms, the adoption of connectivity solutions should free significant time for farmers, which they can use to farm additional land for pay or to pursue work outside the industry.

We find the value of deploying advanced connectivity on these farms to achieve such labor efficiencies represents almost $120 billion, bringing the total value of enhanced connectivity from direct and indirect outcomes to more than $620 billion by 2030. The extent to which this value will be captured, however, relies largely on advanced connectivity coverage, which is expected to be fairly low, around 25 percent, in Africa and poorer parts of Asia and Latin America. Achieving the critical mass of adopters needed to make a business case for deploying advanced connectivity also will be more difficult in those regions, where farming is more fragmented than in North America and Europe.

As the agriculture industry digitizes, new pockets of value will likely be unlocked. To date, input providers selling seed, nutrients, pesticides, and equipment have played a critical role in the data ecosystem because of their close ties with farmers, their own knowledge of agronomy, and their track record of innovation. For example, one of the world's largest fertilizer distributors now offers both fertilizing agents and software that analyzes field data to help farmers determine where to apply their fertilizers and in what quantity. Similarly, a large-equipment manufacturer is developing precision controls that make use of satellite imagery and vehicle-to-vehicle connections to improve the efficiency of field equipment.

Advanced connectivity does, however, give new players an opportunity to enter the space. For one thing, telcos and LPWAN providers have an essential role to play in installing the connectivity infrastructure needed to enable digital applications on farms. They could partner with public authorities and other agriculture players to develop public or private rural networks, capturing some of the new value in the process.

Agritech companies are another example of the new players coming into the agriculture sphere. They specialize in offering farmers innovative products that make use of technology and data to improve decision making and thereby increase yields and profits. Such agritech enterprises could proffer solutions and pricing models that reduce perceived risk for farmers—with, for example, subscription models that remove the initial investment burden and allow farmers to opt out at any time—

likely leading to faster adoption of their products. An Italian agritech is doing this by offering to monitor irrigation and crop protection for wineries at a seasonal, per-acre fee inclusive of hardware installation, data collection and analysis, and decision support. Agritech also could partner with agribusinesses to develop solutions.

Still, much of this cannot happen until many rural areas get access to a high-speed broadband network. We envision three principal ways the necessary investment could take place to make this a reality:

- Telco-driven deployment. Though the economics of high-bandwidth rural networks have generally been poor, telcos could benefit from a sharp increase in rural demand for their bandwidth as farmers embrace advanced applications and integrated solutions.
- Provider-driven deployment. Input providers, with their existing industry knowledge and relationships, are probably best positioned to take the lead in connectivity-related investment. They could partner with telcos or LPWAN businesses to develop rural connectivity networks and then offer farmers business models integrating connected technology and product and decision support.
- Farmer-driven deployment. Farm owners, alone or in tandem with LPWAN groups or telcos, could also drive investment. This would require farmers to develop the knowledge and skills to gather and analyze data locally, rather than through third parties, which is no small hurdle. But farmers would retain more control over data.

How to do it

Regardless of which group drives the necessary investment for connectivity in agriculture, no single entity will be able to go it alone. All of these advances will require the industry's main actors to embrace collaboration as an essential aspect of doing business. Going forward, winners in delivering connectivity to agriculture will need deep capabilities across various domains, ranging from knowledge of farm operations to advanced data analytics and the ability to offer solutions that integrate easily and smoothly with other platforms and adjacent industries. For example, data gathered by autonomous tractors should seamlessly flow to the computer controlling irrigation devices, which in turn should be able to use weather-station data to optimize irrigation plans.

Connectivity pioneers in the industry, however, have already started developing these new capabilities internally. Organizations prefer keeping proprietary data on operations internal for confidentiality and competitive reasons. This level of control also makes the data easier to analyze and helps the organization be more responsive to evolving client needs.

But developing new capabilities is not the end game. Agriculture players able to develop partnerships with telcos or LPWAN players will gain significant leverage in the new connected-agriculture ecosystem. Not only will they be able to procure connectivity hardware more easily and affordably through those partnerships, they will also be better positioned to develop close relationships with farmers as connectivity becomes a strategic issue. Input providers or distributors could thus find themselves in a connectivity race. If input providers manage to develop such partnerships, they could connect directly with farmers and cut out distributors entirely. If distributors win that race, they will consolidate their position in the value chain by remaining an essential intermediary, closer to the needs of farmers.

The public sector also could play a role by improving the economics of developing broadband networks, particularly in rural areas. For example, the German and Korean governments have played a major role in making network development more attractive by heavily subsidizing spectrum or providing tax breaks to telcos. Other regions could replicate this model, accelerating development of connective products by cost-effectively giving input providers and agritech companies assurance of a backbone over which they could deliver services. Eventual deployment of LEO satellite constellations would likely have a similar impact.

Agriculture, one of the world's oldest industries, finds itself at a technological crossroads. To handle increasing demand and several disruptive trends successfully, the industry will need to overcome the challenges to deploying advanced connectivity. This will require significant investment in infrastructure and a realignment of traditional roles. It is a huge but critical undertaking, with more than $500 billion in value at stake. The success and sustainability of one of the planet's oldest industries may well depend on this technology transformation, and those that embrace it at the outset may be best positioned to thrive in agriculture's connectivity-driven future.

Periodical and Internet Sources Bibliography

The following articles have been selected to supplement the diverse views presented in this chapter.

B.R. Cohen, “Why Do Visions of Farming’s Future Never Involve Farmers?” *Slate*. June 20, 2019. https://slate.com/technology/2019/06/robot-farming-futurism-precision-agriculture.html.

Diana Furchtgott-Roth, “Climate Policies Will Shut Down Farmers,” *The Daily Signal*. March 9, 2023. https://www.dailysignal.com/2023/03/09/climate-policies-will-shut-down-farmers/.

Ellie Gable, “The science behind the future of farming,” *SmartBrief*, September 19, 2024. https://www.smartbrief.com/original/the-science-behind-the-future-of-farming.

David Quammen, “Our Desire for Inexpensive Food Is Putting Us in Danger,” *The New York Time*, June 12, 2024. https://www.nytimes.com/2024/06/12/opinion/bird-flu-factory-farming.html.

Andrew Rechenberg, “America’s growing food trade deficit threatens family farms,” *The Washington Times*. February 4, 2025. https://www.washingtontimes.com/news/2025/feb/4/america-growing-food-trade-deficit-threatens-famil/.

Laura Reiley and Kadir van Lohuizen, “Climate change is pushing American farmers to confront what’s next,” *The Washington Post*. November 10, 2023. https://www.washingtonpost.com/business/interactive/2023/american-agriculture-farming-climate-change/.

R.B. Semple, Jr. “America Has a Chance to Make Farming More Climate Friendly” *The New York Times*, June 12, 2023. https://www.nytimes.com/2023/06/12/opinion/climate-change-farm-bill-farmers.html.

Jaskiran Warrik and Shreejit Borthakur, “Farms of the future: How can AI accelerate regenerative agriculture?” *World Economic Forum*, September 10, 2024. https://www.weforum.org/stories/2024/09/farms-ai-accelerate-regenerative-agriculture/.

Chapter 3

What is the Future of Meat?

Chapter Preface

Let's begin with the obvious. To feed the world chicken, millions of chickens must be slaughtered every day. It is safe to say that if the average human omnivore were to witness how chickens are "processed" from living creatures into meat, they might swear off poultry altogether.

Around the world, about 75 billion chickens are processed every year to feed the planet. This necessitates a massive chicken killing industry that operates nonstop. Cows, turkeys, pigs, lambs, and other animals must also be slaughtered in enormous numbers daily in order to satiate humanity's carnivorous appetites.

One does not have to be a radical animal rights activist to think that there might be a better way. Food scientists believe they have come up with one: the invention of cultured meat, which goes by several other names, including lab-grown meat and cultivated meat.

Cultured meat is controversial. Its proponents believe that the meat industry is stripping the planet of its natural resources. They also cite the inhumane practices suggested above. Cultured meat, supporters assert, can put a dent in food insecurity around the globe, feeding millions if not billions.

Others typically believe there is no need for artificial meat. The planet is safe; cultured meat is full of chemicals; fake meat tastes bad; and so on. But even more important for those against this product, cultured meat may impact farmers' bottom line and impede those who depend on raising livestock to make a living.

The battle over cultured meats has already ramped up, with two states, Alabama and Florida, banning the process. Several other states are considering following suit.

This is not surprising. Lab-grown food has always had a certain negative connotation in our society. Science fiction films of the past have depicted artificial food as something sinister. One example is the famous movie, *Soylent Green*. Released in 1973, the film depicts a dystopian, polluted, overpopulated world. Only the rich can afford real meat, and only in scanty portions. The poor are fed lab-created products made by the Soylent Corporation. The general public doesn't know what is in this food. Investigating a murder, New York City Detective Robert Thorn, played by Charlton Heston, discovers the truth. "Soylent Green is people!" he screams into the void in the movie's climatic scene.

But cultured meat is not made of people. Grown in a lab, cultured meat is produced by growing animal cells in a lab environment. Scientists take a small biopsy of cells from a live animal and nurture them in a bioreactor, a large tank that provides the necessary stimulus for cell growth. The cells multiply and separate into muscle, fat, and connective tissues, which are then shaped into desired meat products. This, of course doesn't sound like any food humans have normally eaten, unless one realizes that scientific methodology took over the food industry many years ago. Science is now a driving force in every form of food we eat. Food science already regularly involves the disciplines of chemistry, physics, physiology, microbiology, and biochemistry.

Whether the public at large will gravitate to cultured meat remains unknown. In addition, there are many other factors at play affecting the future of how we consume animal products. The viewpoints in this chapter aim to discuss some of these factors.

VIEWPOINT 1

> *"While it's unlikely livestock farmers are going to begin potty training their herds en masse, interest in biodigesters and pyrolysis systems is growing."*

Innovative Methods are Needed to Combat Livestock-Induced Climate Change

Kristin Houser

In this viewpoint Kristin Houser discusses the environmental impact of meat consumption. To address this challenge, various sustainable alternatives are being explored. Houser emphasizes the urgent need for diverse innovations to lessen the climate impact of meat while promoting ethical and environmentally friendly practices in the industry. Kristin Houser is the Managing Editor of Freethink. Her articles on science and technology have been featured in NBC News, RealClearDefense, and the World Economic Forum's Agenda, among other publications.

"The future of meat is sustainable — and a little weird" by Kristin Houser, Freethink Media Inc., July 30, 2022. Reprinted by permission.

As you read, consider the following questions:

1. According to Houser, what are some of the problems with cultured meat that scientists still need to solve?
2. What methods are researchers exploring that will lead to cows producing less methane?
3. According to the viewpoint, what is pyrolysis and how can it lessen greenhouse gasses?

Humans consume 350 million tons of meat every year — roughly the weight of 1,000 Empire State Buildings — and the figure is expected to climb to more than 550 million tons by 2050 due to a growing world population, rising incomes, and increased consumption per meat-eater.

That's a huge problem for efforts to combat climate change.

Livestock are already responsible for 14.5% of global greenhouse gas emissions. These emissions are mainly generated by producing feed for the animals — tractors, fertilizer, land use, etc. — and by cows themselves, which release the potent greenhouse gas methane from both ends of their digestive tracts.

If we want to meet the demand for meat without further harming our planet, we're going to need to produce it more sustainably. Thankfully, several alternatives to agriculture's status quo are poised to take a place at the dining table of the future.

Growing meat

By creating the right environment around animal muscle cells, scientists can coax them into growing into meat that's molecularly identical to the kind we get from livestock — eliminating the need to raise actual animals.

Printed meat: There's more to meat than just muscle cells, though.

One of the biggest challenges facing the lab-grown meat industry has been replicating the texture of cuts of meat, which contains layers of fat and muscle — and if people can't get lab-grown steak, they'll continue to eat the real kind.

In 2021, Japanese researchers showed how 3D-printing tech could be used to give lab-grown beef the distinct marbling of fat found in Wagyu steaks — opening the door to not only creating steak in the lab, but also custom designing our perfect cut of sustainable beef.

Ethical sausage: Almost all lab-grown meat starts in a culture with fetal bovine serum (FBS), which still comes from animals. But not all.

In July 2022, Dutch biotech company Meatable unveiled a sausage made from lab-grown pork — and unlike the first lab-grown hamburger and most other cultured meat products, the company didn't use FBS to cultivate it.

Because FBS is collected from unborn calves when their mothers are slaughtered, we still need to raise some cattle to obtain it. By eliminating it from the ingredient list, Meatable has made its lab-grown meat more environmentally friendly — and, arguably, more ethical.

Sustainable meat

Exotic meats: Most cultured meat startups are working to replicate pork, poultry, and beef — the most commonly consumed meats — but early-stage UK startup Primeval Foods is thinking wilder, developing lab-grown lion, tiger, and zebra meat.

This focus on exotic creatures might not do much to make traditional agriculture greener, but the opportunity to taste an animal they'd otherwise never find on a restaurant menu could inspire diners who might not bother with lab-grown meat to try it for the first time.

The bottom line: While lab-grown meat is cheaper today than it was in 2013, when it cost $300,000 to grow enough meat for a hamburger, it's still far more expensive than traditional meat, so manufacturers will need to continue to find ways to cut costs while scaling-up production.

They'll also need to navigate regulatory red tape — Singapore is currently the only nation where cultured meat is approved for sale, though experts believe we could see a product on Americans' dinner plates as soon as 2023.

Hacking livestock

To make the future of meat more sustainable, some scientists propose we hack the diets — and genes — of livestock to make them less of a burden on the environment.

Bugging out: Instead of feeding livestock grains — the production of which contributes to deforestation in the Amazon and adds more greenhouse gasses to the atmosphere — Texas State University researchers think we should let the animals dine on insects.

Their research has already shown that the larvae of black soldier flies can be fed to cattle in lieu of traditional protein sources, such as soybean meal, without any noticeable negative effects, and in 2023, they plan to publish a paper detailing how the bug-feed may reduce the animals' methane emissions, too.

Seaweed snack: In March 2021, UC Davis researchers published the results of a study in which a small amount of seaweed was added to the diets of beef cattle.

This seaweed inhibited an enzyme linked to methane production in the animals' digestive systems. As a result, the cattle produced 82% less methane emissions than their standard-diet counterparts. The seaweed didn't affect the animals' weight or the taste of their meat, either.

Sustainable meat

Better breeding: Some cattle seem to naturally produce less methane than others, but no one knew why until 2019, when a team led by University of Aberdeen researchers published a study detailing how genetics strongly influences the makeup of microbes in a cow's gut.

Armed with this knowledge, they say farmers could choose to breed only those animals whose genes make them low emitters — or use gene-editing tech such as CRISPR to quickly make any breed of cattle climate-friendly.

The bottom line: These options would require farmers to rethink how they raise livestock — and, in the case of gene-editing, require greenlights from regulators — but they'd be easier to scale up than lab-grown meat.

Waste not…

Livestock waste is another way meat burdens the environment — manure and urine can both release damaging chemicals into the land and air. Thankfully, some scientists are working on this, let's say, "less-glamorous" aspect of agriculture to make it more sustainable, too.

Waste to fuel: In an effort to make their operations more sustainable — and more profitable — a growing number of livestock farmers are installing "biodigesters" on their farms.

These devices take advantage of microorganisms found in manure to separate it into a liquid fertilizer and several gasses (mostly methane and CO_2).

The fertilizer can be used on a farmer's fields, and the gasses can be used to generate electricity. (Burning the methane, which releases carbon dioxide, is actually still far better for the environment than just releasing it into the air, since methane is a much more potent greenhouse gas.)

MooLoos: When mixed with microbes in soil, cow urine produces nitrous oxide (N_2O), which is even worse than methane. While methane's warming potential is 30 times greater than CO_2, N_2O is 273 times more potent.

With a single cow producing eight gallons of urine a day, the environmental impact of cow wee adds up.

Researchers in Germany and New Zealand recently demonstrated that cows can be trained to urinate in a designated area if given a little encouragement (i.e., a tasty snack). If this discovery could be used to collect even 10% of cow urinations, it could "significantly" reduce greenhouse gas emissions, according to the researchers.

Sustainable meat

Fired up: The idea of heating animal manure to 537 degrees Celsius (1,000 degrees Fahrenheit) might sound incredibly smelly (and surely is), but it can also be a profitable way to make meat production more sustainable.

Researchers from the USDA and the University of Pretoria have developed a mobile system that uses a heating process called "pyrolysis" to convert a farm's manure, grasses, and woody materials into a synthetic fuel that can then be used on the farm, to generate heat or electricity, or sold.

The bottom line: While it's unlikely livestock farmers are going to begin potty training their herds en masse, interest in biodigesters and pyrolysis systems is growing. If the trend continues, the farms of the future could be both more sustainable and more profitable.

Ultimately, we are going to need a huge range of innovations to reduce meat's impact on the climate. But the good news is that researchers are tackling the problem all over the world — and they may end up creating an industry that's safer and more ethical, not just more sustainable.

Viewpoint 2

> *"It took us two years to get our labels approved — because you can add ammonia, you can add all kinds of things to beef or to meat, but as soon as you say you want to add a fresh vegetable, they lose their mind."*

Corporations are Exploring Sustainable Alternatives to Traditional Meat Production

Kara Baskin

In this viewpoint, Kara Baskin also explores the environmental impact of meat production, focusing on how livestock contributes a large portion of agricultural greenhouse gas emissions, particularly from cattle. Baskin notes the strong influence of the meat lobby on regulations and the urgent need for systemic change to reduce the environmental footprint of animal agriculture, advocating for a shift towards plant-based production as a more sustainable solution. Kara Baskin writes the award-winning Parenting Unfiltered newsletter and column for The Boston Globe. *She also writes about food, quirky behavior, and real estate. She has reported and edited for* Boston Magazine, The Boston Phoenix, New York Magazine, *and* The New Republic. *She is the author of* Everything to Everybody: How to Wrangle Kids, Work, Aging Parents, and Spouses When You Just Want to Take A Nap.

"The future of meat" by Kara Baskin, MIT Sloan School of Management, December 22, 2020. Reprinted by permission.

As you read, consider the following questions:

1. According to the viewpoint, why will successful food production companies have to pay more careful attention to labor conditions in the future?
2. Why is marketing so important to the success of cultured meat?
3. According to Pat Brownt, what are some "bogus solutions" to the greenhouse gas dilemma?

There's no doubt that meat is big business, with a significant environmental footprint. As recently as 2017, U.S. meat production totaled 52 billion pounds, 26.3 billion of which was beef. While there are a range of estimates, as much as 30% of the calories consumed globally by humans come from meat products.

And according to the United Nations, livestock contribute nearly two-thirds of agricultural greenhouse gas emissions and 78% of agricultural methane emissions — with cattle representing the bulk of that amount.

Speaking at last month's MIT Sustainability Summit, representatives of five companies discussed ways to reconcile this consumption with eco-friendliness, with various approaches. Speakers included:

- Pat Brown, CEO of Impossible Foods, which develops plant-based substitutes for meat products.
- Charley Cummings, whose Walden Local raises and distributes sustainable meat through a farm-share-like program.
- Jill Marshall Gould, founder of Butter Meat Co., which focuses on mature, organic local beef.
- Cara Nicoletti, whose Seemore Meats & Veggies produces carbon-neutral, vegetable-forward sausages.
- Brian Spears, CEO of New Age Meats, which grows meat from the cells of animals that have not been slaughtered, a process known as "cultivated meat" or "cell-based meat." The company's products are not yet for sale.

While each has a unique business proposition, their hurdles are similar. Here are their insights about the state of the industry.

Human labor is fragile

Panelists discussed how COVID-19 has underscored the frailty of human labor and will remain a topic of concern going forward. Hourly employees who work at slaughterhouses propel the meat supply. Because this work is acutely physical, and conducted in such proximity, it's been difficult for businesses to rely on this labor during the pandemic. Meanwhile, demand surged, underscoring weaknesses in the supply chain.

Savvy companies will be motivated to pay greater attention to workforce conditions in the future. For example, Nicoletti uses data analytics platform Working Metrics, which offers a scorecard to assess and compare how suppliers treat labor, as well as other working conditions.

Cell-based meat could tamp down disease transmission

Futuristic meat companies, meanwhile, hope that their practices will remain unencumbered by disease.

New Age's Spears asserted how conventional meat creation increases disease risk: people in very tight quarters side-by-side, conducting repetitive operations. In contrast, his company creates meat from the cells of unharmed animals.

"A meat supply that relies on humans to be in close proximity to the carcasses of animals and be covered in the fluids of animals presents a transmission risk," he said. "Our platform is fundamentally less prone to that safety risk."

Affordability is a challenge — and a mandate

High-quality meat is also prohibitively expensive for many, which threatens to turn eco-friendly eating into a socioeconomic issue.

"I really want this humane movement to be available to more people," Nicoletti said.

What Is the Future of Meat Consumption?

Driving the demand for animal-based protein

Whether to eat meat and animal-based protein or not is a deeply personal choice. One that is tied to taste, personal beliefs – and the size of your wallet. The correlation between a country's GDP and meat consumption is scientifically well researched, especially as people enter the middle class. Millions of people worldwide are currently making that social move. Per capita, however, meat consumption in mature markets is the highest, with the U.S. topping all other countries.

All this is to say that the demand for animal protein, while already high, is projected to grow steeply into 2030 and beyond. But the future focus of the market will most likely no longer be on the U.S. and Europe. Instead, Asia and Africa will become the driving forces of meat, milk, and egg consumption.

China: Tomorrow's powerhouse of the food market

"China's meat consumption alone is projected to account for 27 percent of the global meat market by 2025," notes Sandra Leible, Market Insights Manager. China's middle class is among the fastest growing in the world; since 2000, the country's gross national income per capita has multiplied more than ten-fold. Just in May this year, China expanded its previous two-child into a three-child policy, a development that may also contribute to a rise in animal protein consumption. "When it comes to milk, China is currently experiencing supply deficiency," shares Gerald Behrens, Head of GSM Ruminants in BIAH.

"The country is working towards ramping up its milk farming operations. At the same time, we observe a longstanding trend to consolidate swine farms to leverage greater efficiencies," he adds. If animal health companies want to make a difference, they will have to place a strong focus on China and other growing economies in Asia and Africa.

Meat or no meat?

Yet as it looks like the trend in meat consumption currently only goes one way – up – a contradictory trend is gaining a foothold in mainstream consumerism: alternative proteins. "The alternative protein market started at a low level but is now experiencing steep growth," Sandra notes.

"At this point, we just don't know how much replacement of meat, dairy, and egg products with alternative proteins there will be. You can observe this trend everywhere in the world to varying degrees. However, it's mostly a phenomenon we see in mature markets." In the end, the choice comes down to consumer preference.

"What is the future of meat consumption?" by Boehringer Ingelheim.

For its part, Impossible Foods has an ambitious goal: completely replace the use of animals as a food source by 2035, with a focus on distribution to malnourished populations. It is estimated that one-third of the world's population is affected by anemia and that half of those cases are due to iron deficiency. As many as two billion people worldwide are iron-deficient.

"It's primarily a problem of poverty. So we have to think about, how do we make these foods more affordable?" Brown asked. He believes that costs will decrease as plant-based meat substitutes become more mainstream.

"We charge more than the animal industry does for our products, but structurally, the economics are all in our favor. This is just a growth phenomenon," he said.

Marketing is key

Mission and method don't move the purchasing needle. Taste does.

"It's really simple. If we make products, we're not going to try to convince people that our mission is a good thing. That's wonderful if they believe that, [but] that's not going to cause people to change their dietary habits," Brown said.

His plant-based Impossible Burger, which mimics the taste of meat, is now in 15,000 grocery stores and 30,000 restaurants worldwide. The company is looking to expand into dairy and seafood. Its product is made from soy protein and heme — an iron-containing molecule that makes the Impossible's meat replicate the real thing. Brown is also considering using leaves as a protein source as a complement to soybeans.

Stressed-out customers might not care much about mission or sourcing, though. Storytelling around brand and provenance has long been part of food companies' marketing strategies, but right now, many people simply want familiar foods and fast.

"People buy meat that they think has the highest quality and tastes the best, and that's what they want to hear first. The environmental case is a box that needs to be checked," said Walden Local's Cummings, acknowledging that messaging might need to change to focus more on flavor.

Two challenges

The democratization of meat might follow the lead of other industries, such as automotive and energy, the panelists said. It will just take time — and government buy-in. The meat lobby is strong.

"It took us two years to get our labels approved — because you can add ammonia, you can add all kinds of things to beef or to meat, but as soon as you say you want to add a fresh vegetable, they lose their mind," Nicoletti said.

"We were blocked at very high levels, to the point where our USDA rep was like, 'I've never seen anything like this.' Because [the industry] is run by meat lobbyists from four major companies," Nicoletti said, referring to behemoths such as Smithfield and Tyson. "We need some help on the government level."

Look to ecological advocacy organizations such as The Good Meat Project to hold greater sway in the coming years, however.

"They're finally getting ears, and there's been some bills introduced in the House … so I think there's kind of a momentum that we can keep going, because customers are looking for it," said Marshall Gould of Butter Meat Co.

The clock is ticking

Meanwhile, greenhouse gas emissions loom large over the industry. Brown emphasized that animal agriculture has devastating environmental impacts, and no amount of refinement can change that.

"Animal agriculture currently exploits 45% of the Earth's land surface, and it's growing. You can see it growing when you watch the Amazon burn. That's centrally entirely driven by a demand for land for animal agriculture," he said. "The total amount of biomass deficit on that land, the delta between what was on that land pre-agriculture and what's on that land now, adds up to the equivalent of about 16 years' worth of current greenhouse gas emissions."

He refused to compromise on what he called "bogus" solutions.

"The stuff about [making] animal agriculture less problematic by feeding them red algae or whatever kind of bull like that, I think is ridiculous. It's the animal agriculture equivalent of clean coal," he said.

He believes the only true solution is replacing the system with plant-based production.

"I don't want to discourage people from trying to make the current system more efficient. But basically, the only way we're meaningfully going to change things is to replace it entirely because it's irreducibly destructive, not just from a climate standpoint, but from a biodiversity standpoint," Brown said.

VIEWPOINT 3

> *"I think what we can all agree on now is the technology is not in a place where it can support a billion-dollar private industry right now."*

Lab Grown Meat as the Future of Food is Still a Long Way Off

Keena Alwahaidi

Keena Alwahaidi writes in this viewpoint about lab-grown meat. While experts acknowledge the environmental benefits of cultured meat, they express skepticism about the technology's readiness for widespread commercial use, with estimates suggesting it may not be available in grocery stores for a many years, even decades. Keena Alwahaidi is a former reporter and associate producer for The Canadian Broadcasting Corporation (CBC). Her interests include news, arts and culture, and human interest stories.

As you read, consider the following questions:

1. According to Alwahaidi, how is lab-grown meat created?
2. According to the viewpoint, why is lab grown meat as a solution to climate change still a long way off?
3. According to Alwahaidi, what issues affect the scalability of cultured meat?

""Lab-grown meat could be the future of food — but possibly not in our lifetimes: experts" by Keena Alwahaidi, CBC/Radio-Canada, February 22, 2024. Reprinted by permission.

What's cultivated, meat-like, and could help lower greenhouse gas emissions? Lab-grown meat — and it could be the future of protein.

Sometimes known as cultured meat, lab-grown meat is unlike plant-based alternatives from companies such as Beyond Meat or Impossible Foods. Instead, it's made by taking a few stem cells from an animal's muscle, then placing them in a nutrient broth where they multiply and are triggered to turn into muscle fibres.

Crucially, it can all be done without killing the animal. Studies have shown that meat production causes nearly 60 per cent of the agriculture industry's greenhouse gas emissions, meaning lab-grown meat could be one of the many answers to climate change reform.

But there's no estimate on when lab-grown meat may hit grocery stores.

Brooklyn-based writer Joe Fassler has spent several years covering the cultured meat industry, and estimates that lab–grown meat might not even be a reality in our lifetimes.

That's because the technology is not all there yet, and recent layoffs have scaled the industry back, he said.

"I think what we can all agree on now is the technology is not in a place where it can support a billion-dollar private industry right now," he told The Current.

Isha Datar, executive director of non-profit research institute New Harvest, agrees that it's hard to get a sense of when we could potentially see lab-grown meat in stores, but still stays on the optimistic side.

"We're seeing enormous climate impacts coming out of farming animals for food," she said. "So we really do need to think about alternative ways to be producing protein for our growing population."

Even if not in her lifetime, she says it's still a worthy cause to pursue — because, if successful, cellular agriculture could potentially "diversify our food system."

And while real meat has effectively fed people worldwide, Datar said the reality of climate change could soon put it out of business.

"We have such enormous densities in some of our farms that it's leading to epidemic viruses being created, such as avian flu and swine flu," said Datar. "And we're seeing enormous climate impacts coming out of farming animals for food."

"We really do need to think about alternative ways to be producing protein for our growing population."

Not a "near-term climate solution"

Fassler says there are other codes to crack to make lab-grown meat thrive.

Cost is one of them, and making this cultivated meat in a way that makes sense economically.

"The challenge here is not to grow the cells. That's been happening for decades in the pharmaceutical industry," said Fassler.

"The issue here is how to reliably grow cells in vast quantities at a cost that makes sense for food. And that's what no one really knows how to do."

The world's first lab grown stem-cell burger is cooked and eaten at a London demonstration

It's true that picking up a piece of lab-grown meat will be pricey. In 2013, the first lab-grown burger patty was made in a Netherlands lab for around $425,000.

And while we could see approvals, Fassler says companies might not be able to keep up making these products at a scale that will feed a large number of people in an economic way.

He said analyses have shown that producing lab-grown meat in large quantities would need large reactors — the vessels where the cells grow and multiply. But most that are large enough aren't currently used to produce cultured meat.

"Imagine these big stainless steel vessels that are over 200,000 litres in volume. And those don't exist for animal cell culture. That's 10 times bigger than the largest reactors the pharmaceutical industry has ever used," he said.

What's more, this won't be a "near-term climate solution," he says.

"This is not going to be a climate solution on a time scale that matters. If we're going to stay below certain critical thresholds in the Paris Agreements, emissions have to decline 43 per cent by 2030," he said.

"If cultivated meat was ready to go now, it would still take that long just to build out the infrastructure that we need."

A bigger idea

Sociologist Neil Stephens, worries that if people view cultivated meat as the perfect answer to climate change, many will stop looking at the bigger picture.

"A big problem here is that it's being represented as a solution — and perhaps as the solution ... which sometimes means that people don't have to think so broadly about other solutions," said Stephens, who is also an associate professor in technology and society at the University of Birmingham.

For now, Datar said new scientific milestones will be more useful than more money in making lab-grown meat more widely available.

Three slabs of steaks

"We're talking about growing something as complicated as tissue and then selling it at a very low volume. So when you think about that, the three billion dollars that has been raised in the field has been spread out amongst 20 plus, maybe even 100 companies."

That's not a lot of money on the biopharmaceutical scale, she said, adding that major scientific advancements often come from "public, government-funded academic routes."

Whatever milestones we reach, Datar is still skeptical about a timeline.

"I don't think this idea of this kind of purist version of meat entirely grown from cells outside of an animal is very feasible in our lifetimes," she said.

"[But] I think we will find something that resembles it... we might find a product on our plate that is mostly plant based with cell cultured elements."

Viewpoint 4

> *"The connection between meat, soy and deforestation might be invisible to consumers, but that link is well known by those in the business of producing and trading both products."*

The Demand for Meat is Driving Deforestation in Brazil

Angela Guerrero and Malika Virah-Sawmy

In this viewpoint, Angela Guerrero and Malika Virah-Sawmy discuss how soy production has led to Brazil's deforestation crisis, noting that the country has become the world's largest soy producer, with much of the crop used as animal feed, especially for European livestock. This expansion has led to the destruction of vital ecosystems. Guerrero and Virah-Sawmy suggest that cooperation between local producers, governments, and international organizations is essential for promoting sustainable soy farming, particularly by using degraded land instead of clearing forests. Guerrero urges consumers to recognize their role in this global dilemma. Angela Guerrero is Postdoctoral Researcher in Environmental Governance at Stockholm University in Sweden. Malika Virah-Sawmy is a Visiting Scientist at Humboldt University of Berlin, Germany.

As you read, consider the following questions:

1. According to the viewpoint, why is soy such a valuable commodity?
2. What are Brazil's regulations regarding deforestation?
3. According to Guerrero, what practices can lessen deforestation?

Soy may have a pretty innocuous reputation thanks to its association with vegan food and meat alternatives. But don't be fooled – crops of this pale legume are behind much of Brazil's epidemic of deforestation. Since 2000, Brazil has doubled its total area of soy plantation to 36 million hectares and become the world's largest producer. This expansion has erased vast swathes of forest and other habitats in some of the country's most biodiverse regions.

About 75% of the soy produced globally is used as animal feed, and a large proportion of soy imported to Europe goes to chicken and pig farms. As a result, the future of the rainforest and savannas of Brazil – not to mention the biodiversity and carbon storage they support – depends on the contents of dinner tables worldwide.

The connection between meat, soy and deforestation might be invisible to consumers, but that link is well known by those in the business of producing and trading both products. Together with colleagues, we investigated this supply chain to find out what's preventing businesses from halting habitat destruction in the Cerrado of Brazil, a tropical savanna where soy agriculture is making inroads.

A lucrative industry

The savannas of the Cerrado surround the westerly borders of the Amazon rainforest. Much of the ongoing deforestation and habitat clearing here is legal – landholders are permitted to deforest up to 80% of their land for agriculture. Clearly, solving this problem isn't a matter of weeding out offenders.

When we spoke with a local association of soy producers, they said that regulation compels them to reserve between 20% and 35% of the Cerrado for nature, but that it's hard to achieve. Asking them to improve on this without compensation would apparently only elicit complaints, and could make landholders more likely to clear habitats from their property while the law still allowed them.

Making demands on Brazilian producers to stop deforesting their land because it troubles European consumers evoked Brazil's colonial past, some argued, and threatened their rights. Soy is seen as a path to national development. Any rules imposed from abroad that threaten this are likely to make matters worse.

Why not compensate people in the Cerrado for producing soy without deforestation? Well, it's not clear who should pay for it. Separating deforestation-free soy from other products would increase the cost for companies sourcing and exporting the soy.

While European retailers sign agreements to end deforestation in their supply chains, implementing them depends on producers and traders cooperating. Retailers argue that passing the cost onto consumers by increasing the price of products like pork is a dead end too. Soy's role in the meat industry is unfamiliar to most people browsing supermarket aisles, so how can consumers be convinced to pay more for a sustainable product they might not understand the benefit of?

Growing soy on deforested land is a very profitable business for those involved, from land speculators looking for cheaper plots at the forest frontier, to the growers and distributors of soy, to the banks financing it. The indigenous communities displaced by expanding farmland are the clear losers. If they fight back, they might be killed.

Such a lucrative business can only be made sustainable if there is a financial case for it. Right now, there isn't. Soy producers are well organised with political clout, and they demand equal partnership in the transition to sustainability, rather than having green rules imposed on them.

Global cooperation for local solutions

Commodities pass between countries and markets in a dense web of exchanges. Data tools are getting better at separating these to reveal the companies and consumer countries linked to deforestation. This recently helped France to reject Brazilian soy, a move which increases pressure on Jair Bolsonaro's government but might mean producers simply supply other markets with lower standards.

Helping soy producers comply with national laws, such as preserving habitats on at least 20% of their property, could help build trust between producers and the people and organisations demanding deforestation-free soy.

This might not sound very ambitious, but even small improvements have been difficult in Brazilian soy agriculture. The Bolsonaro government has slashed the budget for environmental inspectors and signalled to some producers that it's reluctant to enforce national laws. Supporting partnerships between national and state government, and local and international organisations who want to uphold Brazil's own standard could create the necessary trust for enabling bigger changes.

Another option is encouraging farmers to produce on degraded land, rather than seek to convert new forest. Research shows that the amount of land where forest has been cleared could be used to double current soy production. But growing crops on degraded land is actually more expensive than starting it on forested land.

This is where international initiatives can help. The UN Environment Programme and other partners have launched the Responsible Commodities Facility to provide low-interest credit lines to Brazilian soy and corn farmers who commit to using degraded pasture and avoid clearing forests and native grassland for agriculture.

Solutions like this require people in Europe to think beyond their needs – a juicy chicken leg produced without the guilt of deforestation – to consider the values and priorities of people who work to put that chicken on the table in the first place.

Viewpoint 5

> *"If they are using stem cells, cell-based meat companies need to pay attention to the risk of cancer cells emerging in their cultures."*

The Safety of Lab-Grown Meat Is a Serious Concern

Jaydee Hanson and Julia Ranney

In this viewpoint, Jaydee Hanson and Julia Ranney highlight the growing interest in lab-grown meat from numerous companies aiming to create a cleaner and safer alternative to traditional meat, backed by significant investments. However, concerns arise regarding the production methods. These concerns include potential health risks and ethical implications of sourcing animal cells. The authors emphasize the need for transparency in production processes, regulatory oversight, and thorough safety assessments to address potential health risks. In their conclusion, Hanson and Ranney call for rigorous regulations to ensure the safety and integrity of lab-cultured meat as it enters the market. Jaydee Hanson is Policy Director and Julia Ranney is Research and Policy Associate for The Center for Food Safety, an organization whose mission is to empower people, support farmers, and protect the earth from the harmful impacts of industrial agriculture.

"Is Lab-Grown Meat Healthy and Safe to Consume?" by Jaydee Hanson and Julia Ranney, The Center for Food Safety, September 20, 2020. Reprinted by Permission.

As you read, consider the following questions:

1. According to the authors, why are cultured meat companies not being transparent about their methodology?
2. What is a bioreactor?
3. According to the viewpoint, why should lab-cultured meat companies not be allowed to use the Generally Recognized As Safe (GRAS) regulatory loophole wherein they can hire their own experts to evaluate their products?

It goes by many names: cultured, cell-based, cultivated, lab-grown meat, etc. As the names imply, it is a meat alternative made in a lab via animal cells and a cultured medium, like fetal bovine serum or a proprietary mix of sugars and salts. Several companies around the world are promoting this new technique as a way to cultivate a meat alternative that is supposedly "cleaner" and safer than traditional meat.

(We are only looking at those products that culture cells taken from animals into a new meat-like formulation. There are many other products that culture plant, fungi, or algal cells into a meat substitute, but we are not reviewing them here.)

29 companies are planning to bring lab-cultured "meat" to market in the form of chicken, beef, pork, seafood, pet food, and beyond. These companies include Memphis Meats, Aleph Farms, Mosa Meat, Meatable, SuperMeat, and Finless Foods. These companies are backed by huge investments from meat industry corporations (Cargill and Tyson), venture capitalist firms (Blue Yard Capital, Union Square Ventures, S2G Ventures, and Emerald Technology Ventures), and billionaires (such as Bill Gates and Richard Branson).

While the hype is certainly there, is lab-cultured "meat" actually better? Its proponents tout it as an environmentally responsible, cruelty-free, and antibiotic-free alternative to current meat production. While the goal of producing sustainable "meat" without killing animals is admirable, lab-cultured “meat” is in its infancy and the science behind the production methods requires more scrutiny.

Of particular concern is the genetic engineering of cells and their potential cancer-promoting properties. To be able to better assess whether the products are being produced by methods that involve genetic engineering and use genetic constructs (-called onco-genes, typically used to make stem cells keep growing; this is not a problem for lab experiments, but could be for food products-) that might encourage cancer cells, we need more information on how the cells are engineered and kept growing. Many of the companies are claiming this information is confidential and a business secret. These companies are not yet patenting their production processes wherein this information would be more fully disclosed. Some suggest that the production will follow the FDA cell culture guidelines, but the FDA's cell culture guidelines do not apply to this because they're not designed for food.

Lab-cultured “meat” is not always cruelty-free

To produce lab-cultured “meat,” many producers extract animal cells from living animals. This is typically done via biopsy, a painful and uncomfortable procedure that uses large needles. If a company could scale up with this method, it would require a consistent supply of animals from which to acquire cells and innumerable painful extractions. To make the cell-based product more consistent, the producer may biopsy the same animal many times for the cells that growing “meat” requires.

Growing animal cells (typically muscle cells) also requires a growth medium. When lab-cultured “meat” production first began, companies depended on fetal bovine serum (FBS) as a growth medium. Producing FBS involves extracting blood from the fetus of a pregnant cow when the cow is slaughtered.

New methods for scaling up

Given its high cost, it appears that FBS is usually only used during small-scale lab trials. Additionally, increasing production capacity using FBS comes with its own set of concerns. Even disregarding the high cost of FBS, non-genetically engineered animal muscle cells only proliferate or increase to a certain degree. In order to overcome this limitation, large companies such as and Memphis Meats claim they've found an FBS alternative that does not involve animals along with an effective way to expand production. For Memphis Meats, this process involves the utilization of a bioreactor and the creation of immortal cell lines.

These companies are using a bioreactor — essentially a very large vessel for containing biological reactions and processes — to implement a scaffold-based system to grow "meat," which uses a specific structure for cells to grow on and around. The scaffolding helps the cells differentiate into a specific meat-like formation. Researchers cite using cornstarch fibers, plant skeletons, fungi, and gelatin as common scaffold materials. Instead of animal muscle cell precursors (otherwise known as myosatellites), researchers have been using cultured stem cells. This distinction is important because extracted muscle cells will only proliferate to a certain extent. Companies are trying cultured stem cells as an alternative type of cell(s) that could proliferate exponentially so that they could scale up production, and later differentiate the cells into the various cell types that make up animal meat (muscle, fat, and blood cells) in a bioreactor.

In this process, the stem cells still come from animals or animal embryos, but what differentiates the two methods is that in the scaffold-based system, the cells can be genetically engineered to proliferate indefinitely. These cells are otherwise known as pluripotent (which make many kinds of cells, like stem cells) or totipotent (which make every kind of cell, as do embryos). This would greatly expand a company's capacity to make lab-cultured "meat," but the methods by which companies make these cells proliferate come with human health and food safety ramifications.

Human health and food safety concerns about genetically modified cell lines

While the FDA has previously reviewed enzymes, oils, algal, fungal, and bacterial products grown in microorganisms, these new animal cell-cultured products are much more complicated in structure and require a more thorough review. The scale required for making lab-cultured "meat" feasible for mass consumption will be the largest form of tissue engineering to exist and could introduce new kinds of genetically engineered cells into our diets. Further research will also be needed to confirm or dispel uncertainties over various potential safety issues. Candidate topics for research include the safety of ingesting rapidly growing genetically-modifed cell lines, as these lines exhibit the characteristics of a cancerous cell which include overgrowth of cells not attributed to the original characteristics of a population of cultured primary cells. If lab-cultured "meat" enters the market, there are several human health concerns associated with this new production method, specifically that these genetically-modified cell lines could exhibit the characteristics of a cancerous cell.

While these companies don't disclose much to the public about their processing methods, their public patents reveal the creation of oncogenic, or cancer-causing, cells. A Memphis Meats patent on the creation of modified pluripotent cell lines involves the activation or inactivation of various proteins responsible for tumor suppression. Another patent from JUST Inc. describes the utilization of growth factors as part of its growth medium. This process could promote the development of cancer-like cells in lab-cultured "meat" products. Additionally, it is possible certain growth factors can be absorbed in the bloodstream after digestion.

If they are using stem cells, cell-based meat companies need to pay attention to the risk of cancer cells emerging in their cultures. A research team from the Harvard Stem Cell Institute (HSCI),

Harvard Medical School (HMS), and the Stanley Center for Psychiatric Research at the Broad Institute of MIT and Harvard has found that as stem cell lines grow in a lab environment, they often acquire mutations in the TP53 (p53) gene, an important tumor suppressor responsible for controlling cell growth and division. Their research suggests that inexpensive genetic sequencing technologies should be used by cell-based meat companies to screen for mutated cells in stem cell cultures so that these cultures can be excluded.

Cancer-causing additives are prohibited in our food supply under the Delaney Clauses in the 1958 Food Additive Amendments and the 1960 Color Additive Amendments. These new rapidly growing cell lines might be considered color additives Federal Food, Drug, and Cosmetic Act (FFDCA) if they are being used to produce the color in the "meat." The federal statutes regulating meat also prohibit the selling of animals with symptoms of illness, such as cancerous cells in meat. Regardless, all of these new ways of making cells that continue to grow or differentiate should require a safety assessment to determine if they contain cancerous cells before they can be sold.

In describing the scaffolding and growth media being used, lab-cultured "meat" companies need to be fully transparent about what ingredients they're using. During the above-mentioned industry nonprofit's presentation, the presenter suggested the growth media could be composed of a variety of different ingredients like proteins, amino acids, vitamins, and inorganic salts classified under the GRAS (Generally Recognized As Safe) process that allows companies to do their own testing and not submit to a new FDA food additive review. Since companies are not required to fully disclose the composition of their scaffolding or growth media, potentially exposing consumers to novel proteins and allergens, the new mixture of ingredients should be reviewed under a full FDA supervised food additive review, not GRAS.

Another major issue associated with processing methods using cell lines and/or culture medium is contamination. Unlike animals, cells do not have a fully functioning immune system, so there is a high likelihood of bacterial or fungal growth, mycoplasma, and other human pathogens growing in vats of cells. While lab-cultured "meat" companies emphasize that this type of "meat" production would be more sterile than traditional animal agriculture, it's unknown how that is true without the use of antibiotics or some other pharmaceutical means of pathogenic control.

Based on commentary from various companies, antibiotic usage across the industry is still very unclear. While the industry's promoters have outlined many uses for antibiotics in lab-grown "meat" production in preventing contamination, they have not disclosed the amount of antibiotics being used in the various processes. Instead, they suggest that because mass production of lab-grown "meat" will be done in an industrial rather than lab setting, with bioreactors and tanks, there will be higher safety oversight than in medical labs. It is suggested that the many preventative measures in the industry will maintain a sterile boundary and deter antibiotic use in production. It remains a question of how a food production plant would be more sterile than a medical lab.

Companies such as Memphis Meats claim they are genetically engineering cell lines to be antibiotic-resistant, which would suggest they plan on using antibiotics, but don't want their "meat" cells to be affected bacterial and viral contamination plague medical cell culture, so they generally use antimicrobials. Still, any large-scale production that requires antibiotic use even if just for a short-term duration should require such lab-cultured "meat" undergo even stricter USDA drug residue testing, pathogen testing, and FDA tolerance requirements than conventionally-produced meat. Many other companies claim they don't plan to use antibiotics in expanded production which begs the question, in addition to supposed sterile bioreactors, are they using other undisclosed processes to prevent contamination? For example, Future Meat Technologies describes the use of a "special resin" to remove toxins.

The companies have also not disclosed plans for how they will dispose of the toxins from bioreactors, scaffolding, and culture media like growth factors/hormones, differentiation factors, often including fetal calf serum or horse serum, and antimicrobials (commonly added to cultured cells to prevent bacterial and fungal contamination, particularly in). In conventionally-produced meat, animals dispose of these toxins in their urine and feces. If companies can't find a way for this "meat" to dispose of these toxins, the long-term cultures could potentially build up within the "meat" itself. Given the lack of clarity of these companies and their processes, there must be continuous monitoring of the cell lines and growth media/bioreactor for contaminants and some sort of standardization established across the industry to ensure safety.

Final considerations and regulatory recommendations

The industry is new and the exact production process and inputs needed for large-scale, lab-cultured "meat" production are unknown (or not being disclosed by the companies). It is the responsibility of both FDA and USDA to ensure that all inputs used in production and the final product are safe for human and animal consumption. These agencies must ensure that lab-cultured "meat" is labeled appropriately, including if any of the product ingredients are genetically modified or if the ingredients are produced using unmodified cells from animals. These agencies must also ensure that this product doesn't introduce new allergens into the food supply, that any hormones or antibiotics used are not found at unsafe levels in the final product, and that the product doesn't contain any compounds or oncogenic (cancer-causing) cells that have not been approved for use in food.

Lab-cultured "meat" should not be allowed to use the Generally Recognized As Safe (GRAS) regulatory loophole wherein companies can hire their own experts to evaluate their products, often in secret without any notice to the public or FDA. GRAS is an inappropriate designation because the consensus among knowledgeable experts regarding the safety of lab-cultured "meat" does not yet exist. Instead, FDA should require that lab-cultured "meat" products be regulated more thoroughly as food additives. "Meat" companies should submit complete food additive petitions for each of the novel ingredients used to produce these "meats" as well as a final food approval petition for the entire product. The production facilities, like all meat processing plants, should then have USDA inspectors on-site monitoring the process and inspecting the "meat." The USDA announced in August that it will start the process of developing regulations for these new kinds of "meat. Adequate regulation will be necessary to address the concerns raised in this blog.

Overall, due to the novel nature of lab-cultured "meat," the lack of transparency from the companies involved, and the myriad potential health risks to consumers, rigorous regulation of this product is vitally important.

VIEWPOINT

> *"First and foremost, we just got to accept people love meat. And it's difficult, really difficult, to get people to stop eating meat and choose beans or some other plant-based source, which would be better for them."*

Lab-Grown Products Offer a Promising Alternative to Traditional Meat

William Brangham and Mike Fritz

In this interview, the panel discusses the ramifications of the U.S. Department of Agriculture's approval of the production of lab-grown chicken. While this innovation could address environmental concerns associated with meat production, experts express skepticism about its overall sustainability compared to conventional agriculture. William Brangham is an award-winning correspondent, producer, and substitute anchor for the PBS News Hour. *Mike Fritz is the deputy senior producer for field segments at* PBS NewsHour.

"How 'lab-grown' meat is made and will people accept it?" by William Brangham and Mike Fritz, PBS NewsHour, December 27, 2023. Reprinted by permission.

As you read, consider the following questions:

1. Have you ever tried lab-grown meat? If you have, what did it taste like?
2. According to the source, is artificial meat currently more environmentally friendly than traditional meat? Why or why not?
3. According to the source, how close are cultivated meat companies to providing enough product to make a dent in traditional food production practices?

The Department of Agriculture recently approved the production of what's known as cultivated meat, which is chicken grown in a lab. That approval clears the way for companies to begin selling poultry produced from animal cells rather than animals bred in factory farms and killed. But the industry still faces hurdles before Americans see it in their grocery stores. William Brangham reports.

[This is an interview]

Amna Nawaz: Nearly 90 percent of Americans eat meat as a part of their diet. But, earlier this year the Agriculture Department approved the production of what's known as cultivated meat. That is chicken grown in a lab.

That approval clears the way for companies to begin selling poultry produced from animal cells, rather than animals bred in factory farms and killed.

William Brangham gives us a taste of what the future could hold.

Nate Park, Chef, Good Meat: We put a little allium glaze on it, which is just an onion-garlic reduction. Just give it a little color and some flavor on the outside.

William Brangham: At the Good Meat plant in Alameda, California, chef Nate Park is putting the finishing touches on a dish that is seemingly pulled right out of science fiction.

Nate Park: A lot of people don't know what this is. So there's a tendency to maybe back away because they don't know what it is. But I think once they understand what it is, and that it's just chicken, and that it's delicious, it'll be very easy for everyone to get on board.

William Brangham: Getting people comfortable with the idea of cultivated chicken is at the heart of operations here at Good Meat. It's one of two companies now federally approved to make it.

Nate Park: We want to slice it in front of you. We want you to see what it is that you're going to get on the plate.

William Brangham: Grilled, sliced and served with heirloom beans and a sweet potato puree.

If you had said nothing about this, I would just think this was a lovely meal.

Nate Park: Well, thank you.

William Brangham: It tastes, as the saying goes, like chicken.

Nate Park: It's chicken.

William Brangham: And delicious.

Nate Park: Thank you.

William Brangham: But long before I enjoyed it for lunch today, that chicken meat could only be seen here, inside this bioprocessing lab, as tiny microscopic stem cells.

They're all taken from real chickens without harming them. The cells are then constantly stirred, kept warm, and nourished, so that they will multiply inside these massive bioreactors.

It's all part of a lengthy process designed to mirror how actual animals grow.

Josh Tetrick, CEO, Eat Just: Cultivated meat has been talked about for over 100 years.

William Brangham: Josh Tetrick is the co-founder and CEO of Eat Just, which operates Good Meat.

What is the rationale for cultivated meat?

Josh Tetrick: First and foremost, we just got to accept people love meat. And it's difficult, really difficult, to get people to stop eating meat and choose beans or some other plant-based source, which would be better for them.

So how do you get at that? And I think the answer is, you make real meat in exactly the same taste and texture that people are used to, but you make it in a way that doesn't require billions of animals. You just can't feed the world without the billions of animals, because each animal has to be slaughtered.

William Brangham: Global food production is responsible for roughly a third of all the manmade greenhouse gases that are dangerously heating the planet. And meat production is the major driver of that impact, with the majority of the world's croplands and forests being used to grow food for the animals we then eat.

Josh Tetrick: If were going to solve the climate problem, we definitely need to move from fossil fuels to renewable energy. And we also definitely need to move from intensive animal farming that is eating up a third of our planet today to an entirely different approach.

William Brangham: But not everyone is sold on this new approach.

Ned Spang, University of California, Davis: We can't just take it as a given that cultured meat is good for the environment.

William Brangham: Ned Spang is an associate professor at the University of California, Davis, who studies the links between food and the environment.

He says, while no animals are being slaughtered, a recent report he co-authored about cultured meat indicates it's not nearly as green as many would hope.

Ned Spang: Along the lines of climate emissions or energy use, we found that cultivated meat might actually have more of an impact than the conventional agriculture.

William Brangham: And how is that possible?

Ned Spang: Well, the major driver is that these are still animal cells, so they still need to eat food. And, basically, just as a cow needs to eat some grass or corn to grow and grow muscle mass, we need to feed the cells. And so we need to feed them glucose for energy and amino acids to build proteins.

And it takes a lot of resources to actually make the food to grow these cells to create the cultivated meat.

William Brangham: But Tetrick argues that, as the technology improves, cultivated meat has the potential to pollute much less and consume far less land and water than conventional meat.

And he argues, our current approach, from its cruelty to animals to its environmental impacts, has to change.

Josh Tetrick: We're eating food every day that no one would be proud of if they actually engaged with it.

William Brangham: Several companies have come to market with plant-based meat substitutes, like Beyond Meat or Impossible Burgers.

But cultivated meat will likely be a tougher sell. A recent poll from the Associated Press found that half of adults in the U.S. say they would be unlikely to try it, with many citing that it sounded weird.

Josh Tetrick: We found the most effective way to move someone from, this is kind of weird to, all right, I'm down with it, is put it on a plate, get them hanging out with their friends and have them eat the chicken. And then a bit about midway through it, they're like, all right, this is just chicken.

William Brangham: So far, only a few restaurants in the U.S. have actually served cultivated chicken, including China Chilcano in Washington, D.C.

William Brangham: Take it right like this?

Daniel Lugo, Head Chef, China Chilcano: Yes. Don't be afraid to get a little messy. No worries.

William Brangham: That is delicious.

It's owned by world-famous chef Jose Andres, and here, head chef Daniel Lugo prepares it as a traditional Peruvian street food.

So when Jose first came to you and said, we'd like to try cooking with this unique type of chicken, what was your reaction?

Daniel Lugo: Well, at first, I was super excited and curious. And, to be honest, once I tried it, I was super surprised and actually liked it.

William Brangham: But getting cultivated meat both into more restaurants and eventually into grocery stores won't be easy.

Good Meat is reportedly looking for ways to cut surging production costs. The company had aimed to eventually produce up to 30 million pounds of meat annually.

Josh Tetrick: Yes, we are nowhere near the scalability to actually make a dent in this problem. And that was exactly the same way for solar energy 30 years ago. And we were in exactly the same position for electric cars 20 years ago.

And if you're ultimately going to shift the system, best to start now, because it's going to be a many-many-decade long, very, very hard, uncertain problem to solve.

William Brangham: It's a problem now being tested and tasted in labs like this one.

Viewpoint 7

> *"From a food security perspective, cultured meat offers a way to diversify protein production to help meet the global population's nutritional needs."*

Cultured Meat Offers a New Role for Traditional Farms

Innovation for Agriculture

This viewpoint, derived from a webinar, discusses the emergence of cultured meat as an alternative protein source and its potential effects on livestock farming in the United Kingdom. The authors note that while cultured meat could disrupt certain sectors, such as poultry and beef production, it may also create new opportunities for farmers, particularly in supplying raw materials for its production. The viewpoint identifies specific types of farms that may be most affected, both positively and negatively, by the rise of cultured meat. Innovation for Agriculture connects farmers with farming research. They work with leading agricultural researchers, businesses, landowners, and farmers to develop the knowledge and technologies that will make modern farming more sustainable, resilient, and productive.

"How will cultured meat impact farming?" by Innovation for Agriculture, March 30, 2023. Reprinted by permission.

As you read, consider the following questions:

1. According to Professor Marianne Ellis, what is cellular agriculture?
2. According to the viewpoint, how can the lab-grown meat industry still offer opportunities for traditional farmers?
3. What did you learn from this viewpoint about lab-grown meat that you did not learn from others in this chapter?

Growing cultured meat as an alternative protein source will impact livestock farming, threatening some sectors and causing disruption to others, but will likely create opportunities for some farm businesses too.

A recent webinar hosted by Abi Kay from Farmers Weekly shared the findings from a research project which explored farmers' thoughts about cultured meat, led by the Royal Agricultural University.

What is cultured meat?

Speaking in the webinar, Professor Marianne Ellis from University of Bath shared that cultured meat is one of the products from cellular agriculture.

She explained that cellular agriculture is a collection of technologies which use alternative methods to produce consumables traditionally produced in livestock-based agriculture systems.

Examples of cellular agriculture include:

- Using yeast in precision fermentation to make oils and fats, which can be used as palm oil substitutes
- Using mycelium, which is effectively the root structure for fungi, to make an alternative protein. For example, this is how Quorn is made
- Growing muscle cells, which are referred to as cultured meat, lab-grown meat or cultivated meat

In its basic form, cultured meat is a protein ingredient made up of muscle cells only. A longer-term goal is to grow 'full cut' cultured meat, with the complex structure that results from combining the different cells which occur in 'natural' muscle, such as nerves, blood cells and connective tissue.

How is cultured meat grown?

Cultured meat is grown by taking biopsies from recently killed animals in the food chain – to provide stem cells, from which the muscle cells can grow. A cell culture media also needs to be added to supply nutrients for the growth of the muscle cells, this is essentially a broth containing the required nutrients. The process takes three to four weeks.

Is cultured meat needed?

From a food security perspective, cultured meat offers a way to diversify protein production to help meet the global population's nutritional needs.

Currently 790 million people do not have access to enough food. The global human population stands at about 7.7 billion and is forecast to grow to 9.8 billion by 2050. The additional protein required to feed the extra 2.1 billion people, at an average of 50 to 80g per person per day, amounts to an extra 105 to 168 million tonnes of protein per year.

However, as raised by some farmers in the discussion groups during the research process, and by speaker Evan Roberts during the webinar, food waste is a significant global problem, and much of the shortfall in food could be met by resolving the issues which lead to food wastage.

What opportunities does cultured meat offer to farmers?

Putting aside the uncertainties around how well it will resolve food security issues, the farmers in the focus groups informing the research identified some potential opportunities that cultured meat offers to UK farmers.

The opportunity to supply the raw materials for cultivated meat. At the moment, raw materials are being purchased from research companies, but if/when cultured meat is approved for sale in the UK there will be opportunities for UK farmers to supply both the food grade stem cells from traditionally reared livestock and the raw materials for the nutrient broth mixture, which could be waste materials from local farms.

The introduction of cultured meat products to supermarkets could lead to a strengthened USP for grass-fed livestock and on-farm production of meat.

The idea that cultured meat could be produced on farms was discussed and not completely ruled out, although mostly deemed unlikely.

It was recognised that there is a need for gamechangers and disruption in UK farming, to spark the innovations and solutions to effectively respond to global challenges like climate change. Cultured meat could be a game changing technology.

What threats does cultured meat pose to farming in the UK?

Several threats and concerns were raised in the discussions which informed the research. These included:

- Impacts on specific sectors - cultured meat could displace demand for the chicken going into chicken nuggets or the beef from dairy cull cows used to make burgers
- Disruption to carcase balance - livestock don't just produce meat, many food and cosmetics products are reliant on co-products from livestock. Reducing livestock numbers could rebalance the value of co-products
- Possible undercuts to animal welfare - if cultured meat production develops to the point where it is cheaper to produce than farm reared meat, it is possible that animal welfare could be compromised
- Negative impact on rural economy – there are areas of the UK where farmed livestock contribute to creating a sense of

FDA Clears Lab-Grown Chicken as Safe to Eat

Lab-grown chicken has taken a step closer to hitting American grocery stores.

The Food and Drug Administration on Monday cleared cultured "cultured chicken cell material" made by GOOD Meat as safe for use as human food. While the FDA said the lab-grown chicken was safe to eat, GOOD Meat still needs approval from the Agriculture Department before i can sell the product in the U.S.

If approved, acclaimed chef José Andrés plans to serve GOOD Meat's chicken to customers at his Washington, D.C. restaurant. He's on GOOD Meat's board of directors.

"The future of our planet depends on how we feed ourselves," he said in a press release. "And we have a responsibility to look beyond the horizon for smarter, sustainable ways to eat."

The FDA previously gave the green light to lab-grown chicken made by Upside Foods in November.

Upside Foods and GOOD Meat both use cells from chickens to create the cultured chicken products.

Once cells are extracted, GOOD Meat picks the cells most likely to produce healthy, sustainable and tasty meat, the company explained. The cells are immersed in nutrients inside a tank. They grow and divide, creating the cultured chicken, which can be harvested after four to six weeks.

"It's real, delicious meat with an identical nutritional profile to conventionally raised meat but with less impact on our planet and less risk of contamination," GOOD Meat said on its website.

GOOD Meat's chicken is already sold in Singapore.

Global livestock accounts for nearly 15% of greenhouse gasses, the Food and Agriculture Organization of the United Nations found in 2013. Advocates for lab-grown meat say it can help cut back on methane emissions and combat climate change.

"FDA clears lab-grown chicken as safe to eat" by Aliza Chasan, CBS Interactive Inc., March 21, 2023.

place, which attracts tourism. If livestock were to be removed from these areas and the landscape changed, the local rural economy would likely be affected

- Consolidation of power in food supply chain – growing cultured meat will likely put protein production into the hands of a smaller number of companies who own the technology, shifting the balance of power in the food system
- Nutrition and health – although protein content of cultured meat has been shown to be the same as meat from animals, other micronutrients such as 'B' vitamins will need to be added into the product. There were concerns around nutrient equivalence and also whether cultured meat will contribute to increased consumption of highly processed food products, which could be detrimental to human health
- Disconnection from food – there were concerns around the impact of cultured meat on consumers' understanding and connection with the food they eat. One farmer described cultured meat as 'the perfect vehicle for further disconnection from food'

Which farms will be most affected by cultured meat in the UK?

The research so far has identified eight farm profiles that are most likely to be affected by cultured meat – both positively and negatively. These are:

- Large-scale pig/poultry
- Conventional beef/lamb
- Pasture-fed/organic livestock
- Rare breed livestock
- Dairy
- Fruit/vegetables
- Arable
- On-farm food processing/brewing

Periodical and Internet Sources Bibliography

The following articles have been selected to supplement the diverse views presented in this chapter.

Alice Callahan, "Is Fake Meat Better for You Than Real Meat?" *The New York Times*, Feb. 17, 2025. https://www.nytimes.com/2025/02/17/well/eat/is-fake-meat-healthy.html.

Jack Hubbard, "Lab-grown meat is a loser among Republicans, Democrats," *The Washington Time.* June 3, 2024. https://www.washingtontimes.com/news/2024/jun/3/lab-grown-meat-is-loser-among-republicans-democrat/.

Jon Jackson, "The Future of Meat Is Here—Straight From a Lab," *Newsweek*, December 2, 2020. https://www.newsweek.com/lab-made-meat-approved-1551898.

Eduardo Porter, "To Save the Planet, Stop Eating Free-Range Beef," *The Washington Post*, January 14, 2025. https://www.washingtonpost.com/opinions/2025/01/14/free-range-beef-climate-change/.

Katherine Rampel, "Don't chicken out of eating lab-made meat. It could change the world.," *The Washington Post*, October 1, 2024. https://www.washingtonpost.com/opinions/2024/10/01/lab-grown-meat-taste-test-chicken/.

Somini Sengupta, "Our Taste for Flesh Has Exhausted the Earth," *The New York Times*. September 21, 2024. https://archive.ph/SZEW8#selection-791.2-795.15

Matt Spence, "The National Security Case for Lab-Grown and Plant-Based Meat," *Slate*, December 29, 2021. https://slate.com/technology/2021/12/plant-cultivated-meat-national-security.html.

Chapter 4

Will Food Continue to Be Used as a Weapon of War?

Chapter Preface

According to contemporary international law, starvation of a civilian population is "a war crime, a crime against humanity, and an act of genocide." The tactic is as old as war itself, but it is less commonly acknowledged than, say, nuclear weapons, or chemical warfare. This may be because starvation is a long, slow process. It doesn't fit neatly into a news cycle.

Food scarcity continues to be used as a method to control and kill civilians in the 21st century. The Israeli-Palestinian conflict is one example of the tactic. However, according to Oxfam, "Most wars of the late 20th and early 21st centuries have been 'food wars': food and hunger were used as weapons, food and food-related water and energy infrastructure were damaged intentionally or incidentally, and food insecurity persisted as a legacy of conflict destructiveness." Oxfam estimates that in 2023, the denial of food in conflict situations led to between 7,784 and 21,406 deaths per day. The Russia-Ukraine conflict is responsible for many of those deaths, but ongoing conflicts causing food deaths are also occurring in Ethiopia, Nigeria, Somalia, Syria, and Yemen, to name but a few.

In an Op-ed entitled "Food May Be the Ultimate Weapon in the 21st Century," Hal Brands, Senior Fellow at the American Enterprise Institute, warns that Vladimir Putin's war on Ukraine could have major consequences on the global food supply going forward: "A ruthless tyrant is squeezing the world's food supplies in hopes of isolating and then conquering his neighbor. The U.S. and other leading democracies haven't figured out how to solve that problem — which may be a preview of the way that food and conflict will increasingly interact in a fragmenting world.

The viewpoints presented in this chapter detail different perspectives on how food supplies will be affected by conflicts in the future.

Viewpoint 1

"Famine is a very specific political product of the way in which societies are run, wars are fought, governments are managed. The single overwhelming element incausation—in three-quarters of the famines and three-quarters of the famine deaths—is political agency."

Political Actions are the Chief Cause of Famine

Heather Stephenson

In this interview conducted by Heather Stephenson, author Alex de Waal discusses the historical context and decline of famines, asserting that while mass starvation has significantly decreased since the 1930s, the underlying political causes remain critical. He expresses concern about the current global political climate, which may hinder progress in combating famine effectively. Heather Stephenson is the editor of Tufts Magazine, *the university's alumni magazine, and produces stories for all Tufts channels, with a special focus on The Fletcher School of Law and Diplomacy. Before joining Tufts in 2012, she was editor-in-chief at the Appalachian Mountain Club, an editor at* Our Bodies Ourselves, *and a staff and freelance journalist.*

"Mass Starvation as a Political Weapon" by Heather Stephenson, TuftsNow, January 18, 2018, Reprinted by permission.

As you read, consider the following questions:

1. Why does Alex de Waal argue that famine is primarily a political issue rather than a natural calamity?
2. What "loopholes" are used by nations to avoid the label of war crimes when it comes to starving a population?
3. Why has de Waal lately become less hopeful about ending starvation?

Mass starvation killed more than three million people in Stalin-era Ukraine in the 1930s and more than 18 million in China during Mao Zedong's Great Leap Forward in the late 1950s and early 1960s. Yet by the start of this century, famines like those were all but eliminated, Alex de Waal says in his new book, *Mass Starvation: The History and Future of Famine*. The number of people dying in famines around the world has dropped precipitously, particularly over the last thirty to fifty years.

Those gains, though, are fragile, and could be starting to be reversed, says de Waal, who is the executive director of the World Peace Foundation and a research professor at the Fletcher School. For his book, he compiled the best available estimates of global famine deaths from 1870 to 2010, and used that data to analyze trends. *Tufts Now* sat down with him recently to find out what he learned.

***Tufts Now*: In the popular imagination, famine is often connected with too many people and too little food—that is, with overpopulation and low agricultural production due to natural disasters such as drought. How does that line up with reality?**

Alex de Waal: That is nonsense. Famine is a very specific political product of the way in which societies are run, wars are fought, governments are managed. The single overwhelming element in causation—in three-quarters of the famines and three-quarters of the famine deaths—is political agency. Yet we still tend to be gripped by this idea that famine is a natural calamity.

You can actually show that the population theory of famine is wrong. Not just wrong at a global scale—because famine mortality has gone down precipitously while world population has gone up—but also at a country level. In the countries that have historically been very prone to famine, like Ethiopia or India, famine mortality has gone down and continues to do so even while population goes up. This is not to say that there isn't a problem of resource consumption in the world. It's just to say famine is not part of that.

You say that mass starvation was almost eliminated, with famines becoming less frequent and less lethal. How did that happen?

There are multiple reasons: the background economics, the improvements in transport systems, information systems, massive improvements in public health. The big historic killers in famines used to be infectious diseases. Those are now much less likely to kill large numbers of people.

One big factor is the international humanitarian industry. The humanitarians are much better at addressing the symptoms than the causes. But nonetheless if you can reduce the lethality of famines to a small fraction of what they used to be twenty, thirty, fifty years ago, even if you're not addressing the causes, you're still doing something substantially positive.

The last reason for the decline in famines is undoubtedly the decline in wars, the decline in totalitarian rule, and the spread of democracy and liberal values. There's something very tangibly precious to be held onto about democracy, liberalism, and humanitarianism. You can demonstrate that this has saved tens of millions of lives. It shouldn't be treated lightly.

In addition to sending humanitarian aid, outsiders have sometimes argued for intervening with military force to protect

civilians who are suffering during famines in conflict zones. What do you think of that?

I think it's a terribly bad idea—it's very likely to go wrong. Twenty-five years ago, when President Bush the elder sent his troops to Somalia, I resigned from Human Rights Watch over it. I was asked to support it, and I refused. I still think it's a bad idea. Almost every instance where you see troops sent in, it has not worked out well. These are not problems that can be solved by the military.

You say that the success in combating famine is now stalling and that world leaders should help by making the act of starving people a war crime or a crime against humanity. Isn't it already against international law?

Lawyers will argue about this. Some will say there is no law that outlaws faminogenic acts—acts that create famines—and there are so many loopholes in international law that you can fly fighter jets through it, as the Saudis are doing now in Yemen. Others will say the law is there if interpreted correctly.

What can't be denied is that it's an issue that we collectively don't care enough about to make the criminalization work.

Let me give a parallel, which is sexual and gender crimes. Rape has always been unlawful, but it was only relatively recently that the international community—global public opinion—cared enough about criminalizing rape to actually make it into an issue that could be stopped. In the same way, I think we need to care enough about starvation, in places like Yemen, Syria, Nigeria, and South Sudan, to make it an issue that is so toxic that it is stopped.

You mention Yemen, where an ongoing armed conflict and blockade imposed by a Saudi-led coalition have left millions in need of humanitarian assistance. What should be done about the people starving there?

Yemen is the greatest famine atrocity of our lifetimes. The Saudis are deliberately destroying the country's food-producing infrastructure.

The United States and the European countries, if they cared about it enough, have enough leverage to get the Saudis and the Emeratis to stop bombing agricultural, health, and market infrastructure, open the ports, and have a much less restrictive definition about what food is allowed in. They also need to start a peace process. This is not a war that is going to be won in any meaningful sense. It's a political, created famine and it will have to be solved by political, created means. One can ameliorate the impact by enabling a humanitarian response, which would save many lives, and allowing the economy to regenerate a bit, but a proper solution has to be a political one.

How hopeful are you about the possibility of ending famine?

At any time up to a couple of years ago, I would have been extremely hopeful. The default mode of the national and global governance systems was in favor of humanitarian systems and against faminogenic actions. That was the way history was going. That was the direction of global politics.

Now I'm much less certain about that, as we are seeing some of this introverted, xenophobic, transactional, zero-sum politics. It's not just here in the U.S. You also see it in Europe, with Britain as a particularly sad example.

Humanitarianism cannot cope with the political causes of famine. Humanitarians know that. But there's still an assumption by political leaders, who are somewhat culpable, that if we put the humanitarians on the case, we don't need to deal with the politics. That is wrong.

> *"The importance of politics and diplomacy is key in order to end wars that have a devastating impact on the lives of civilians. The various parties must commit to complying with international humanitarian law, which prohibits attacks on food and civilians. "*

Hunger Is a Brutal Weapon

Ulriikka Myöhänen

Ulriikka Myöhänen discusses the severe impact of war and conflict on global food security. She observes how conflicts, such as the ongoing war in Ukraine and crises in Sudan and Gaza, disrupt access to sufficient and nutritious food for civilians. Myöhänen observes that food is often used as a weapon in warfare, with attacks on food supplies and agricultural resources leading to starvation and malnutrition, particularly among vulnerable populations. She also calls for international cooperation and adherence to humanitarian laws to protect civilians and restore food systems in conflict-affected areas. Ulriikka Myöhänen is a humanitarian communications specialist, journalist and managing editor.

"Hunger is a brutal weapon – wars in Ukraine, Sudan and Gaza significantly undermine global food security" by Ulriikka Myöhänen, Finn Church Aid, November 28, 2024. Reprinted by permission.

As you read, consider the following questions:

1. What are the four main dimensions of food security as defined by the World Food Summit?
2. How has the war in Ukraine impacted global food security and prices?
3. According to Myöhänen, what humanitarian issues are have affected food access in Gaza and Sudan?

Food should not be used as a tool of war, yet conflicts affect people's access to sufficient and nutritious food. In recent years, alongside local challenges, the world has witnessed a unique phenomenon: the war in Ukraine, now in its third year, has affected food security worldwide.

Critical food aid lifelines into northern Gaza severed
Starvation in war-hit Sudan "almost everywhere".
Russian missiles hit two grain ships in the Black Sea.

These headlines are excerpts from the international media and UN agencies in September-October 2024. A quick glance at the news will tell you a few important things:

Firstly, war always affects the food supply of ordinary people. Secondly, even in today's wars, the control of food and its associated resources is the weapon which affects civilians the most.

The actions behind the headlines – such as bombing, destruction of farmland and water resources, and sabotage of food shipments – are horrific acts not only from the perspective of civilians struggling in the midst of conflicts, but also because they strongly undermine the international rules-based order.

International humanitarian law is a set of rules that seeks to limit the effects of armed conflict. It clearly states that starvation of civilians is absolutely prohibited as a method of warfare. It is also forbidden to attack objects that are essential to the survival of the civilian population. These may include food, grain fields, crops, livestock, water supplies and irrigation systems.

The rules of war are constantly being violated. In 2024, we still live in a world where children are starving to death, missiles and rockets are destroying food supplies, and food aid is not reaching civilians living in the midst of devastating conflict.

In developing regions, wars are often fought in areas that already suffer from a lack of adequate food and livelihoods, such as limited pasture and cropland. Food and disputes over food can therefore be both a tool of warfare and a cause of conflict.

Food is a human right

The right to food is a right of every human being.

According to the World Food Summit held in 1996, food security is achieved when "all people, at all times, have physical and economic access to sufficient safe and nutritious food to meet their dietary needs and preferences for an active and healthy life."

There are four main dimensions to food security. Food must be available: it must grow in fields and be stored. To achieve food security, people must also have access to food. In other words, they must be able to buy or produce food for themselves and their families.

In addition to being available, food must be nutritious and varied so that people's energy and nutrient needs are met. The fourth dimension is the stability or permanence of food security. Good quality and nutritious food must be available from day to day and people must have access to it for an individual to be considered food secure. Political instability, extreme weather conditions, rising prices and unemployment can all affect stability around food security.

Up to a third of the world's food ends up as waste

Today, food security is not achieved for everyone, even to the extent that food is available at all. According to a recent report by the Food and Agriculture Organization of the United Nations (FAO), one in 11 people in the world and one in five on the African continent will go hungry in 2023 – this despite the fact that the world produces more food than people can eat.

It is estimated that at least a fifth or even a third of the food produced goes to waste. In rich countries, too much food is bought and then left uneaten. In the poorest countries, food is wasted already at harvest time due to inadequate storage facilities and markets.

The past few years have been exceptional in terms of the deterioration of global food security. This is due to the Covid pandemic and Russia's war of aggression in Ukraine.

Coronavirus began spreading around the world from the Chinese city of Wuhan in December 2019. The viral disease, which became a pandemic in the spring of 2020, closed borders and significantly limited people's interactions and daily life.

The pandemic had an impact on nutrition, food security and food systems, i.e. the whole that consists of food production, processing, distribution and consumption.

Covid also had a significant impact on food chains, i.e. how raw materials end up on people's tables through processing, handling, distribution and sale. The effects were global due to the lockdowns and restrictions during the pandemic and the sickening of those working in the sector.

Additionally, the pandemic also forced people to change their eating habits, as informal markets that often sold cheap vegetables to families, especially in developing countries, were closed due to restrictions on gatherings. Social programs that helped the poor could no longer provide food assistance in the same way as before.

Many lost their livelihoods, which meant that families had less money to buy food. At the same time, as the pandemic progressed, food prices rose significantly.

In 2022, the world was hit by a new global crisis, this time starting on the European continent. Russia's war of aggression in Ukraine has proven how interconnected the world we live in is.

Ukraine is a major European breadbasket, with agricultural products reaching tables around the world in recent years. The country is located on the Black Sea, through which significant amounts of grain, cooking oil and fertilizers are transported to the world.

When the war began, Russian warships in the Black Sea blockaded Ukrainian ports, thus closing trade routes. Energy and fuel prices rose. Food exports from Ukraine to the world suffered significantly before transport across the Black Sea was restored, at least partially, and alternative routes were found for Ukrainian agricultural products through European countries.

Ukrainians have lost their fertile farmland to invading forces, and the fields have become minefields. The fields themselves and the crops they grow have been completely destroyed in some places. Those who still farm are struggling to grow crops in the midst of war. There is a shortage of electricity due to ongoing attacks on energy infrastructure.

Transporting food from farms to international consumers has become significantly more difficult due to closed trade routes, ongoing security threats, and increased transportation costs.

The war in Ukraine and its impact on food security have been felt across the world, from Central America to the Middle East and Asia. The war caused global food prices to reach record highs in March 2022, but have since fallen to pre-pandemic levels.

The Covid pandemic and the war in Ukraine have been visible on family dinner tables around the world. But think about this: many people in the developed world buy a bag of highly processed bread from a store, the price of which consists of the shares received by the producer, the food industry and the store, as well as VAT. The share of raw materials – and the price change that has occurred due to the global market – is ultimately just a small everyday expense in our breakfast rolls.

In poorer countries, instead of buying ready-made rolls, people buy a big bag of raw materials, grain, from which they grind flour at home, for example, for a month's needs. The price of wheat on the world market is reflected more painfully in the monthly expenses of a low-income family and also in the price of breakfast bread than in richer families.

Attacks on grain ships and food production continue in Ukraine

Despite the rules of war, Russia has used food as a weapon of war in Ukraine repeatedly, forcefully, and for a long time.

The war in Ukraine has been going on for almost three years, and yet attacks on grain ships, grain warehouses and food production continue. Although markets have managed to at least partially compensate for the lack of Ukrainian products on world markets, the war is already having, and will continue to have, long-term effects on food security.

The effects have already hit those who were already most hungry. As prices have risen, organizations have also had fewer food aid resources at their disposal. This means that fewer and fewer families dependent on food aid in crises around the world are getting enough food on their plates.

FAO predicts that up to 600 million people will be chronically malnourished in 2030. If the COVID-19 pandemic and the war in Ukraine had not happened, there would be up to 119 million fewer people undernourished in 2030. The war in Ukraine alone affects the forecast by 23 million people. Chronic malnutrition is hitting Africa hard, where people are already living in famine.

THE LAST few years have brought turbulence to the big picture of food security, but there are also many regional and local crises in the world today that are significantly undermining food security.

Of all of them, the most difficult has received the least attention. More than half of Sudan's population – 25 million people – will be acutely food insecure when the country enters civil war in 2023.

New Commentary Urges Policy to Combat Rising Food Weaponization

Because of the interconnected food systems of today's globalized world, the use of food as a weapon of war is more dangerous than ever, and few tools exist for governments to deter the deadly practice, according to a recent commentary in Foreign Affairs, one of the country's most celebrated and influential foreign policy magazines.

The piece calls for the creation of a new global ban on food weaponization to curb the deliberate disruption, destruction, and manipulation of critical food supplies as a method of warfare.

Zachary Helder, who just graduated from the Princeton School of Public and International Affairs with a Master in Public Affairs, is one of the five co-authors of the article, "Food Weaponization Makes a Deadly Comeback." The others are former U.S. Secretaries of Agriculture Mike Espy, Dan Glickman, and Mike Johanns, and the former global head of corporate affairs at Cargill, Devry Boughner Vorwerk.

The commentary argues that since its invasion of Ukraine, Russia has taken the longstanding and widespread weaponization of food to "a new level" by making one of its military objectives the disruption of the global food supply. Moscow's actions include bombing granaries in Ukraine, imposing export restrictions, and blockading the Black Sea.

"In an interdependent global economy, food weaponization in one region could affect the food security of all," the authors write.

Helder, who previously served as a senior adviser for food and agriculture policy in the U.S. House of Representatives, hopes the piece will spark a conversation that results in real action.

"Food weaponization is a resurgent but ancient problem that has become much more dangerous in a globalized world, a reality which I think has been slow to set in," he said. "For my co-authors, who are widely known and respected voices in food and agriculture, to offer this big idea — a novel treaty framework — means that the piece could make a real difference."

The authors argue a new framework is necessary because the West currently does not possess an effective means to deter

> food weaponization on a global scale. In their opinion, international humanitarian law, maritime law, existing trade agreements — and even the Geneva Conventions — all fall short. To remedy the situation, they envision a treaty that would specify in clear terms that no legitimate military purpose exists for attacks on the means of production or distribution of food.
>
> **"New Commentary Urges Policy to Combat Rising Food Weaponization" by Adam Grybowski, The Trustees of Princeton University, August 01, 2024.**

A famine has already been declared in the North Darfur region, which is also home to a camp for 500,000 internally displaced people. International organisations agree that hunger is currently the main cause of suffering among Sudanese civilians.

The warring factions in Sudan are also using hunger as a weapon of war. According to reports, the conflict parties are severely destabilising food systems, causing mass displacement and systematically destroying livelihoods. The parties are also blocking food aid from reaching the opposing territories.

The situation is also very serious in Gaza, where civilians are not getting enough food due to continuous airstrikes. Israel is also severely restricting the adequate access of food aid to Gaza.

There are also reports that food aid reaching the Gaza Strip has been looted. Israel blames the looting on Hamas, the Islamist extremist organization that controls Gaza. Organising food aid is currently difficult, also because Gaza is under constant bombardment and evacuation orders, and it is not possible to organize food storage and distribution safely.

It has long been known that Gaza is in a food security emergency that could soon turn into an outright famine. In October 2024, three-quarters of the population of the Gaza Strip is completely dependent on food aid, the limited farmland has been destroyed by bombing, and food supplies on the market are scarce and, as a result, very expensive.

How will food security be restored?

The World Food Programme Estimates that there are now as many as 71 countries facing acute hunger. The situation is most serious in Sudan and Gaza, but hunger is also seen in countries such as South Sudan and Mali. The hunger crisis has also been prolonged in Somalia, which first suffered from a historically long drought and then from rains that have caused devastating floods in the country.

In addition to conflicts and economic shocks, climate change is a significant factor increasing food insecurity. Conflicts, lack of livelihoods and climate change, in turn, force people to leave their homes. The cycle repeats, as displacement also significantly increases human food insecurity.

So what can be done to ensure that everyone has bread on their plate in the future? The most informed guesses emphasise cooperation; in which governments, financial institutions, the private sector, and sectors responsible for humanitarian work and development cooperation improve food security.

The importance of politics and diplomacy is key in order to end wars that have a devastating impact on the lives of civilians. The various parties must commit to complying with international humanitarian law, which prohibits attacks on food and civilians.

And finally, as the dust settles on the battlefields, it will be time to look to the future and think about how people will be able to return to their farms to produce food and earn a living.

Viewpoint 3

> *"Reducing access to food to attack the morale and will of a group to resist is not always successful in terms of creating the environment for victory or deterrence."*

Weaponization of Food Doesn't Always Result in Victory

Greg Kennedy

In this viewpoint, Greg Kennedy discusses the critical humanitarian crisis in Gaza, where over half a million residents have faced catastrophic hunger as a result of the conflict between Israel and Hamas, made worse by Israeli measures that restricted food access as part of an aggressive military strategy. Kennedy explores the historical context and tactical implications of using starvation in warfare, citing examples such as past sieges that demonstrate its effectiveness in weakening an opponent's morale and physical ability to resist. He suggests that using hunger as a weapon may ultimately backfire, though. The tactic can unify adversaries against the aggressor nation and damage its moral standing in the global community. Greg Kennedy is Professor of Strategic Foreign Policy and Director of the Corbett Centre for Maritime Policy Studies at King's College in London.

As you read, consider the following questions:

1. According to the viewpoint, what is a "siege"?
2. What are some famous examples of aggressor countries using food as a weapon of war?
3. How can the tactic of using food as a weapon motivate its victims, according to Kennedy?

More than half a million Gazans are currently facing "catastrophic hunger", according to UN agencies. Reducing access to food is being used as a weapon in Gaza by the Israeli government.

Denying food to a civilian population is a tactic that has been used in conflicts for centuries. Starvation and malnutrition provide the attacker with a number of advantages. At the tactical level the enemy is denied mobility, is unable to sustain law and order among its population as vital foodstuffs become scarce, and the will to fight diminishes. Also the physical ability to fight is likely to erode.

Weakened bodies become susceptible to disease, while fear and hopelessness are enhanced due to the body's inability to provide the brain with required nutrients. Fighters watch their families suffering and this can create doubt and guilt in their minds.

There are similarities between Israel's tactic and the way strategic bombing in the second world war and the allied blockade of Germany in the first world war aimed to make the civilian population unwilling to support their government's war effort. Drastically reducing access to food is a punitive and indiscriminate attack on the morale and will of an opponent.

Restricting food reaching the people of Gaza is a strategy sometimes called deterrence by punishment. Weakening Gazans by limiting their access to food, as well as conducting bombing raids, allows the Israelis to conserve their conventional land forces in case the conflict escalates and those forces are required to face other enemies.

The strategy also signals to potential adversaries the severe actions and levels of commitment Israel is prepared to go to in search of victory, and to rebuild the image of Israel's ability to defend itself, which was damaged after the October 7 attacks.

Sieges in history

Sieges are typically associated with an aggressor encircling a defender, and controlling access to a city with implications for food supply. One of the earliest recorded sieges, a military operation to force the population to give up control, was the battle of Megiddo in present day Israel, during the 15th century BC.

Egyptians besieged the city for seven months. The city's name when translated from Hebrew gives us the modern word armageddon, meaning a terrible battle that may lead to the destruction of the world.

Another example is the battle for the Spanish city of Ceuta. Believed to be the longest siege in history, it lasted 26 years. The Moroccans eventually took the city in 1720, but it was recaptured when Spain brought in thousands of reinforcements.

In more modern times, when Germany attacked the Soviet Union during the second world war it laid siege to the former imperial capital of Leningrad (now St. Petersburg). German forces cut off the city for 872 days. Very few supplies got through to Leningrad until January 1943, and the city itself would not be relieved until January 1944. It is estimated that 630,000 people died of hunger.

Starvation is a powerful tool on the battlefield, producing crippling and destructive effects as efficient in many ways as bombing, though it takes longer for the necessary effects to take place.

At the strategic level the fear of starvation, disease and civil breakdown creates a powerful deterrent. The idea of women and children indiscriminately being subjected to the horror of conflict weighs heavily in the mind of leaders of conflicts, often causing doubt and disunity.

Sellers of foodstuffs and tradespeople fear disruption to their trade and economic welfare, bringing even more pressure to bear on those leaders to acquiesce and find a peaceful solution, even if it means compromise and strategic defeat. Images and stories of humans starving to death evoke primal emotions, which have a powerful effect on policy and decision making in times of conflict.

This attritional siege-like strategy is used to avoid costly losses to a state's own forces in unfavourable terrain or conditions, such as urban warfare, mountain warfare, jungle warfare or having to retake large areas of territory with limited land forces.

Reducing access to food to attack the morale and will of a group to resist is not always successful in terms of creating the environment for victory or deterrence. Aggressors sometimes gain control of a city or area for a short time only, as was true in Stalingrad.

The use of food as a weapon, in Gaza represents the same dangerous double-edged sword it has throughout history.

The tactical action can create the motivation for previously divided or splintered groups to come together in the face of unspecific and general terror. Neutral parties, and allies, can view depriving women and children of food as being indicative of a state or group that is not to be associated with, causing a loss of the moral high ground. That momentum can gather pace and build alliances between those who wish to defeat any nation that would wield such an indiscriminate weapon.

And as far as deterring other future acts of aggression, the use of food as a weapon may only create future enemies, or at the very least, alienate friends.

Viewpoint 4

> *"The hungry people of the world are counting on us...and we must not let them down."*

Peace Is the Only Way to Prevent Famine in War-Torn Countries

The United Nations

This viewpoint by United Nations officials highlights the urgent need for action to address severe food insecurity in conflict-affected countries. They suggest that violence and conflict are major contributors to widespread hunger, with millions at risk of famine in places like Yemen, South Sudan, and Ethiopia. Key figures, including the Under-Secretary-General for Humanitarian Affairs and the Executive Director of the World Food Programme, stress the importance of political solutions to end conflicts and the necessity for increased humanitarian funding. The authors also call for a focus on long-term strategies to build resilience against food insecurity, linking climate action with peacekeeping efforts, and ensuring that vulnerable populations receive the support they need to survive. The United Nations is an international organization founded in 1945. Currently made up of 193 Member States, the UN and its work are guided by the purposes and principles contained in its founding charter.

As you read, consider the following questions:

1. Can you name other examples of places around the world where lasting peace might make for a more food-secure future?
2. What is the role of conflict in worsening food insecurity according to Máximo Torero?
3. What actions were suggested for UN member states to support economies facing severe, large-scale hunger?

Dire food insecurity in many conflict-affected countries requires both urgent action from the Security Council to prevent and end the violence and increased humanitarian funding from the international community in order to avert catastrophic famine for millions of people, senior United Nations officials told the 15-member organ today.

Martin Griffiths, Under-Secretary-General for Humanitarian Affairs and Emergency Relief Coordinator, recalled that the Council asked to be informed when the risk of conflict-induced famine and widespread food insecurity occurs. "That risk is now upon us," he reported. Widespread suffering was a result of the direct and indirect impacts of conflict and violence — along with the behaviour of the fighting parties. In the most extreme cases, such actors deliberately cut off access to the commercial supplies and essential services on which civilians rely to survive. "Hunger is used as a tactic of war," he stressed.

Providing a brief overview of the bleak situations in Yemen, South Sudan, Ethiopia and north-east Nigeria — where a total of approximately 43 million people face high levels of food insecurity — he offered several suggested actions for Member States to take. These include pursuing peaceful, negotiated resolutions to conflict and supporting the economies of countries facing severe, large-scale hunger, among others. Further, these countries receive little — if any — funding for climate adaptation and mitigation. He called on Member States to ensure this funding reaches the most vulnerable places as a matter of priority. "Time is not on our side," he stressed.

Máximo Torero, Chief Economist of the Food and Agriculture Organization (FAO), underscored that conflict impacts every aspect of agrifood systems, reducing food production, destroying crops, disrupting markets and restricting access to food. In the long term, it leads to complete loss of livelihoods, mass displacements and decreased resilience, among others. Detailing the dire food security situations in Somalia, Afghanistan, Ethiopia, South Sudan, northern Nigeria and Yemen, he pointed out that: "When the Council speaks, the world listens." Preventing conflict is the most effective means of preventing famine. "It is essential that we act now to minimize the calamities," he stressed.

David Beasley, Executive Director of the World Food Programme (WFP), said that up to 345 million people are "marching towards starvation" in the 82 countries where the WFP currently operates, and of those, 50 million people living in 45 countries are "knocking on famine's door". Echoing previous assessments of the bleak situations in Ethiopia, north-east Nigeria, South Sudan and Yemen, he urged the Council to "show the leadership the world needs right now" and help facilitate political solutions to end these wars. Recalling his April 2020 warning that the world was facing "famines of biblical proportions", he stressed that "we are on the edge once again". "The hungry people of the world are counting on us," he added, "and we must not let them down."

In the ensuing discussion, many Council members expressed concern over food insecurity in Ethiopia, north-east Nigeria, South Sudan and Yemen, calling for peaceful solutions to armed conflict and welcoming the Black Sea Grain Initiative's impact on lowering global food prices, while others stressed that Russian fertilizer must also be able to reach global markets. Some also stressed the need to take a more long-term approach, urging efforts to address underlying causes of food insecurity and build resilience in vulnerable countries.

On that point, the representative of Brazil, who, along with Ireland, requested this meeting, stressed the need to break the perverse cycle formed by conflict and food insecurity that traps people in a spiral of degrading living conditions. Efforts were needed to eradicate historical trade-distortive practices. While donor countries must ensure that no humanitarian agency needs to choose between the hungry and the starving, he also urged all Member States to increase their efforts in providing technical capacity and technology.

Ireland's representative, also pointing out that United Nations agencies and non-governmental organizations are being forced to take food from the hungry to feed the starving, stressed that this is a "damning indictment of the state of food insecurity globally, and of this Council's response to conflict-induced hunger". Humanitarian assistance is essential, but it is not the answer to this scourge, he stressed. Rather, the solution is peace, which means putting pressure on the parties to conflict to come to the table.

The representative of Kenya said, however, that, while food insecurity may be most acute in conflict-affected countries, it is a broader phenomenon. He therefore urged relevant States, regional bodies and United Nations entities to refocus on Sustainable Development Goal 2 on zero hunger. Further, there is sufficient evidence that the climate crisis aggravates conflict. The Council needs to heed the call by countries in the Sahel and the Horn of Africa to link climate action with the peacekeeping and political missions of the United Nations.

Similarly, the representative of the United Arab Emirates called on the international community to help combat climate change by prioritizing investments in early warning systems, anticipatory action and agricultural resilience. Recalling that her country has consistently advocated for taking more unconventional drivers of conflict into account, she said the Council would be better able to take preventative action to address worsening security and humanitarian situations if it received regular updates on risk factors in fragile settings.

Also addressing the Council was Italy's representative, who stressed that the international community must maintain open food chains and transition towards sustainable, climate-smart and resilient food systems. "Rural people and local actors must be put back at the centre of these processes," he stressed.

Periodical and Internet Sources Bibliography

The following articles have been selected to supplement the diverse views presented in this chapter.

Lauren Baker, "Food systems transformation in a time of global conflict," *The Global Alliance for the Future of Food*, May 6, 2022. https://futureoffood.org/insights/food-systems-transformation-in-a-time-of-global-conflict/.

Barbara Celis, "The day the UN barred using hunger and starvation as weapons of war," *World Food Programme*, May 24, 2022. https://www.wfp.org/stories/un-barred-using-hunger-and-starvation-weapons-war.

Alex de Waal, "Hunger as a Weapon: A war strategy from Sudan to Gaza," *World Peace Foundation*, October 15, 2024. https://worldpeacefoundation.org/blog/hunger-as-a-weapon-a-war-strategy-from-sudan-to-gaza/.

Laura Del Duca, "Food Insecurity: A Weapon of War?" *Siani*, October 8, 2024. https://www.siani.se/blog/food-insecurity-a-weapon-of-war/.

Zach Helder, Mike Espy, Dan Glickman, Mike Johanns, and Devry Boughner Vorwerk, "Food Weaponization Makes a Deadly Comeback, *Foreign Affairs*, March 22, 2024. https://www.foreignaffairs.com/ukraine/food-weaponization-makes-deadly-comeback.

Birgit Kemmerling, Conrad Schetter, and Lars Wirkus, "The logics of war and food (in)security," *Global Food Security*, Volume 33, June 2022. https://www.sciencedirect.com/science/article/pii/S2211912422000256?via%3Dihub.

Ore Koren, "Food, Climate Change, and War in the 21st Century," *Georgetown Journal of International Affairs*," April 21, 2023. https://gjia.georgetown.edu/2022/03/07/food-climate-change-and-war-in-the-21st-century/.

Oxfam, "Food Wars: Conflict, Hunger, and Globalization, 2023," *Oxfam*, October 2024. https://oxfamilibrary.openrepository.com/bitstream/handle/10546/621657/bp-food-wars-241016-en.pdf.

Michael N. Schmitt, "Weaponizing Food," *Articles of War*. March 28, 2022. https://lieber.westpoint.edu/weaponizing-food/.

Amanda Taub, "Israel, Gaza and the Law on Starvation in War," *The New York Times*, May 4, 2024. https://www.nytimes.com/2024/05/04/world/middleeast/israel-gaza-starvation-icc.html.

Ishaan Tharoor, "The world's 'worst crisis' is in Sudan," *The Washington Post*. March 3, 2025. https://www.washingtonpost.com/world/2024/12/04/sudan-hunger-crisis-civil-war-famine-starvation/.

For Further Discussion

Chapter 1

1. After reading the viewpoints in this chapter, do you think the world is capable of feeding its entire population?
2. In your opinion, how serious is the threat of climate change on the future world food supply?
3. Why do you think it is so difficult to feed the planet going forward when an abundance of food exists?

Chapter 2

1. After reading the viewpoints in this chapter, what do you believe is the future of the family farm?
2. After reading the views presented, do you believe that corporate farming is the way of the future?
3. After learning more about them, how do you feel about new technologies aiding future farmers?

Chapter 3

1. After reading the viewpoints in this chapter, would you consider eating lab-grown meat? Why or why not?
2. After exploring different points of view, do you think that lab-grown meat can help reduce the affects of climate change?
3. Do you lab-grown meat can help solve food insecurity in the future? Which viewpoints would you use to support your argument?

Chapter 4

1. After reading the viewpoints in this chapter, do you believe that using food as a weapon is a war crime? Why or why not?
2. Do you agree with the old saying that "all's fair in love and war"? Why or why not?
3. After reading viewpoints in this chapter, what do you think should be done about countries that use food insecurity as a weapon?

Organizations to Contact

The editors have compiled the following list of organizations concerned with the issues debated in this book. The descriptions are derived from materials provided by the organizations. All have publications or information available for interested readers. The list was compiled on the date of publication of the present volume; the information provided here may change. Be aware that many organizations take several weeks or longer to respond to inquiries, so allow as much time as possible.

Action Against Hunger

1 Whitehall Street
2nd Floor
New York, NY 10004
(877) 777-1420
info@actionagainsthunger.org
https://www.actionagainsthunger.org/

Action Against Hunger is a global humanitarian organization which originated in France and is committed to ending world hunger. The organization helps malnourished children and provides communities with access to safe water and sustainable solutions to hunger. Across more than 55 countries, Action Against Hunger reaches 21 million people a year through their lifesaving and life-changing hunger programs.

The American Farm Bureau Federation

(202) 406-3600
info@fb.org
https://www.fb.org/

The American Farm Bureau Federation is the voice of agriculture in the United States. The organization is comprised of farm and ranch families working together to build a sustainable future of safe and abundant food, fiber, and renewable fuel for the United States and the world.

Cato Institute

1000 Massachusetts Avenue NW
Washington, DC 20001
(202) 842-0200
www.cato.org

The Cato Institute is a libertarian public policy research organization, a think tank dedicated to the principles of individual liberty, limited government, free markets, and peace. Its scholars and analysts conduct independent research on a wide range of policy issues, including issues related to food and food security.

Center for American Progress

1333 H Street NW
10th Floor
Washington, DC 20005
(202)-682-1611
www.americanprogress.org

The Center for American Progress is a public policy research and advocacy organization which presents a liberal viewpoint on economic and social issues, including issues related to how we grow and consume food. Their website includes a range of articles on various social issues.

Feeding America

161 North Clark Street
Suite 700
Chicago, IL 60601
(800) 771-2303
https://www.feedingamerica.org

In 2024, the Feeding America network distributed 5.9 billion meals through programs like mobile pantries and Kids Cafes to help people in local communities get the food they need to thrive. Feeding America works with food companies and farmers to supply food banks with food that would otherwise go to waste. In 2022 alone, the Feeding America network rescued 4 billion pounds of food and groceries.

Future Food Institute

Piazza Giuseppe Verdi, 2,
40126 Bologna BO
Italy
+39 051 656 9619
info@futurefoodinstitute.org
https://futurefoodinstitute.org

The Future Food Institute exists to sustainably improve life on Earth through education and innovation in global food systems.

The Global Alliance for the Future of Food

info@futureoffood.org
https://futureoffood.org

The Global Alliance for the Future of Food was founded in 2012 with the aim of transforming food systems now and for future generations. They are a strategic alliance of philanthropic foundations that work together to leverage our resources and networks to help shift food and agriculture systems toward greater sustainability, security, and equity. The Global Alliance has witnessed the power of partnership to achieve positive change. Food systems transformation requires new and better solutions at every level. The Global Alliance aims to achieve such a transformation through ideas that take a systems-level approach and involve deep collaboration between the philanthropic sector, researchers, grassroots movements, private sector stakeholders, farmers and food systems workers, Indigenous peoples, governments, and policymakers.

The United Nations

760 United Nations Plaza
New York City, N.Y. 10017
(212) 963-4475
https://www.un.org/en/contact-us-0
https://www.un.org

The United Nations is an international organization founded in 1945. The UN has evolved over the years to keep pace with a rapidly changing world, and it remains the one organization on Earth in which all the world's nations can gather together, discuss common problems, and find shared solutions that benefit all of humanity.

The World Bank

1818 H Street NW
Washington, DC 20433
(202) 473-1000
https://www.worldbank.org

The World Bank is a multinational organization whose mission it is to create a world free of poverty on a livable planet. This goal is threatened by multiple, intertwined crises. To achieve its goals, the World Bank works in close partnership with other multilateral institutions, the private sector, and civil society. A key focus of their efforts is food insecurity.

World Farmer's Organization

Via del Tritone, 102,
00187 Rome
Italy
+39 06 421291
info@wfo-oma.org
https://www.wfo-oma.org/

The World Farmers' Organisation (WFO) is a member-based association, bringing together national farmers' organizations and agricultural cooperatives from all over the world. WFO's mission is to represent the farmers' voice and advocate on their behalf in all the relevant international processes affecting their present and their future, ranging from the global discussion on agriculture to nutrition and sustainability.

Bibliography of Books

Muṣṭafá Bayram and Çağlar Gökırmaklı. *The Future of Food*. Newcastle upon Tyne, UK: Cambridge Scholars Publishing, 2020.

Bālakr̥shṇa, editor. *Sustainable Agriculture for Food Security: A Global Perspective*. Palm Bay, FL: Apple Academic Press; CRC Press, 2022.

Darin Detwiler. *Building the Future of Food Safety Technology: Blockchain and Beyond*. Amsterdam, Holland: Academic Press, 2020.

Nina Guilbeault. *The Good Eater: A Vegan's Search for the Future of Food*. New York, NY: Bloomsbury Publishing, 2024.

Julie Guthman. *The Problem with Solutions: Why Silicon Valley Can't Hack the Future of Food*. Oakland, CA: University of California Press, 2024.

Will Harris and Amely Greeven. *A Bold Return to Giving a Damn: One Farm, Six Generations, and the Future of Food*. New York, NY: Viking, 2023.

Kevin Kurtz. *The Future of Food*. Minneapolis, MN: Lerner Publications, 2021.

Scott Lively. *For the Love of Beef: The Good, the Bad and the Future of America's Favorite Meat*. Vancouver, BC: Page Two, 2021.

Ian Mosby, et al. *Uncertain Harvest: The Future of Food on a Warming Planet*. Regina, Saskatchewan, Canada: University of Regina Press, 2020.

Lenore Newman. *Lost Feast: Culinary Extinction and the Future of Food*. Toronto, Ontario, Canada: ECW Press, 2022.

Meredith Sandland and Carl Orsbourn. *Delivering the Digital Restaurant: Your Roadmap to the Future of Food*. Herndon, VA: Amplify Publishing, 2021.

Jorg Snoeck and Stefan Van Rompaey. *The Future of Food: A New Recipe for the Food Sector*. Translated by Ian Connerty, Lannoo Campus, Leuven, Belgium, 2021.

Chloe Sorvino. *Raw Deal: Hidden Corruption, Corporate Greed, and the Fight for the Future of Meat*. New York, New York: Simon Acumen, 2022.

Karl Weber, editor. *Food, Inc. 2: Inside the Quest for a Better Future for Food*. New York, NY: PublicAffairs, 2023.

Timothy A Wise. *Eating Tomorrow: Agribusiness, Family Farmers, and the Battle for the Future of Food*. New York, NY: The New Press, 2019.

Index

A

agtech, 53, 55–56
animal agriculture, 103, 120
artificial meat, 89
autonomous machines, 78–79, 82

B

beef, 93–94, 98, 102, 115, 133, 135
Beyond Meat, 105, 128
biodiversity, 29–30, 44, 58–59, 61–63, 65, 68, 103, 110

C

canning, 70
cattle, 93–95, 98
cellular agriculture, 106, 111, 131
climate change, 23–27, 29–31, 36, 44–45, 75, 92, 105–107, 133, 152, 160
Climate Change Action Plan, 32
Clustered Regularly Interspaced Short Palindromic Repeats (CRISPR), 16, 95
Community Supported Agriculture (CSA) programs, 68–69, 71
connectivity, 74–80, 83–86
consumable food calories, 23, 25–27
COVID-19, 29, 35, 76, 99, 147–149
crop
  failure, 30, 55
  rotation, 65, 67
cultivated meat, 98, 106–107, 124, 126–128, 131, 133

D

deforestation, 45, 94, 110–113
dehydrating, 70
DNA, 14–16
drones, 78–79, 81–82

E

ecosystems, 44–45, 68, 83, 85

F

famine, 59, 140–143, 149, 151, 158–159
farmer's market, 65, 69, 71–72
farm subsidies, 51, 58–63
farm-to-table movement, 67
Federal Food, Drug, and Cosmetic Act (FFDCA), 119
fertilizer, 14

fetal bovine serum (FBS), 93, 115–117
"Flavr Savr" tomato, 14
Food and Water Watch, 17
food
deprivation, 27
insecurity, 17, 20–21, 27, 29, 34–39, 42, 46, 89, 138, 149, 152, 158–160
prices, 29–30, 35–36, 147–148, 159
security, 17, 20, 23, 26, 29–30, 32, 34, 36–37, 39, 46–47, 59, 132, 145–149, 151–152, 159
shipments, 145
supplies, 15, 23, 119, 121, 135, 138, 144, 146, 151, 155
weaponization, 150–151
fossil fuels, 126
"Frankenfoods," 15
freezing, 70

G

Generally Recognized As Safe (GRAS), 119, 121
genetically modified organisms (GMOs), 14–15, 17
genetic engineering, 14, 17, 116
Good Meat Project, 102
greenhouse gas emissions, 29, 53, 62, 66, 68, 92, 94–96, 98, 103, 105, 126
grocery stores, 20, 26, 65, 69, 72, 102, 105, 124, 128

H

harvests, 20, 26, 44, 66, 72, 80–81, 146
healthy diets, 35–36, 39, 44
herbicide, 55
human labor, 99
human rights, 44, 146

I

Impossible Foods, 98, 101–102, 105, 128
Intergovernmental Panel on Climate Change, 26
irrigation systems, 31, 146

L

lab-grown food, 89, 92–93, 95, 105–107, 115, 118, 120, 131, 134
livestock, 46, 54, 76–80, 89, 92, 94–96, 98, 131, 133, 135, 146
locally sourced produce, 64–72

M

malnutrition, 34, 36–39, 41, 44, 149, 154
manure, 95–96
methane, 29–30, 92, 94–95, 98
Monsanto, 15

N

nutrition, 34–39, 44–46, 132, 135, 147

O

oilseeds, 60, 63

P

Paris Agreement, 31, 107
pesticides, 14, 53, 65–68, 82–83
plant-based meat substitutes, 101–102, 128
pollution, 44–45, 58
pork, 93, 111, 115
precipitation, 23–24
pyrolysis, 96

R

rainforests, 110
renewable energy, 126
rice paddies, 31

S

savannas, 110
Save Family Farming, 50
siege, 155–156
slaughterhouses, 99
soil degradation, 58
soybeans, 23, 26, 94, 102
sustainability, 27, 32, 34, 37–39, 44, 46, 53, 55, 65–69, 71, 74–76, 79, 86, 92–96, 98, 111–112, 115, 160–161
starvation, 138, 140–142, 145, 154–155, 159
State of Food Security and Nutrition in the World (SOFI Report), 34, 39
Syngenta, 15

T

technology, 15–17, 31–32, 38, 46, 50–51, 53–56, 74–84, 86, 104–105, 107, 115, 119–120, 127, 131, 133, 135, 160
temperature, 23–24, 30, 80
transporting food, 46, 65–68, 141, 148

U

undernourishment, 27, 41–42, 149
U.N. Environmental Programme, 112
U.N. Food and Agriculture Organization, 27, 34, 36–37, 39, 147, 149, 159
U.N. Food Systems Summit (UNFSS), 45, 47
United Nations Children's Fund (UNICEF), 39
U.N. World Food Programme, 34, 39, 152, 159

U.S. Department of Agriculture (USDA), 20, 50, 96, 102, 120–122

U.S. Food and Drug Administration (FDA), 14, 116, 118–122

W

war, 17, 145–149, 151–152, 154–156, 158–160

water supply, 30–31, 44–45, 75, 146

weather, 23–24, 29–30, 55, 75, 77, 80, 85, 146

Z

zero hunger, 34, 36, 40–41, 45, 160